Timeless
Principles
of
Exceptional
Businesses

TIMELESS PRINCIPLES *of* EXCEPTIONAL BUSINESSES

Shared Wisdom from 25 Years of TAB

TAB

THE ALTERNATIVE BOARD

Shared Wisdom, Bottom Line Success

Direct Communication Service, Inc.

Timeless Principles of Exceptional Businesses

Published by Direct Communication Service, Inc.

Copyright © 2015 by TAB Boards International, Inc.

Direct Communication Service, Inc.
11031 Sheridan Blvd.
Westminster, Colorado USA 80020

Printed in the United States of America.

2015 — First Edition

Book cover and interior design: AuthorSupport.com

Special pricing for bulk sales is available.

Please email marketing@thealternativeboard.com for more information.

CONTENTS

ACKNOWLEDGEMENTS

O ne of the things that made creating this book an enjoy-able and invigorating process was the willingness of so many talented people to contribute to it. At TAB we sometimes speak of the "community model of business," where businesses are collectively stronger by working together. This was a true community effort involving many long-term members and TAB facilitator / coaches.

I want to especially thank Katie Fritchen for being the primary organizer and editor on this complex project. Katie turned this project from a rough idea into a definitive project. She conducted the interviews with long-term members and facilitator / coaches. She provided significant content and editorial contributions across all the content and is the major reason this book now exists. I also want to thank Dave Scarola for his leadership, content contributions and project management input to this effort.

I want to thank the authors from the TAB community who contributed chapters to this book. Their names and titles are located within each chapter. They took the time to provide their salient insights into what makes companies special, which has resulted in a series of interesting and insightful articles.

My gratitude goes to Dana Besbris for organizing the key contacts for the production of this book and for providing detailed review and editing of multiple revisions of this content. In early brainstorming sessions about how we should recognize our 25th anniversary, it was Dana who came up with the idea of "25 Business Insights from 25 Years". Without that idea, this book would not have happened. I also want to thank Jodie Shaw for joining this project and making very strong editing contributions that added the necessary polish and professionalism to this book.

I would like to provide a very special thanks to a handful of long-term TAB members who shared their insight into the evolution of business over the past 25 years and their insights into the qualities it takes to run exceptional businesses, like their own. Specifically, Mark Abels of Custom Time Corporation, Eric Aschinger of Aschinger Electric, Michael Benker of Banner Fire Equipment, Lynn Gastineau of Gastineau Log Homes and Thom Noller of Mayfair Liquors.

We also conducted interviews with long-term and former TAB facilitator / coaches who provided their insight on business changes and the timeless principles of exceptional businesses. Thank you to Wayne Berry, John F. Dini, Jim Marshall, Jim Strohan and Bill Vrettos.

I appreciate the efforts of Jennifer Mabry, my dedicated line editor, and Jerry Dorris, who provided expert cover design and interior layout. Jennifer edited early versions of chapter content and added a significant level of consistency and quality to the content of this book. Jerry provided fantastic cover design, content layout and production presenting this content in the best possible light.

I want to thank Jason Zickerman, CEO of TAB, for his continued leadership and passion for The Alternative Board. TAB has become a truly global organization under Jason's leadership and I am delighted that TAB Boards are now available to business owners in so many countries.

Finally, a very special thank you for all of the current and former TAB members and facilitator / coaches who have been part of the TAB system at some time over the past 25 years. It's been an honor and a pleasure to be affiliated with you.

INTRODUCTION

A quarter century ago, I had a dream of developing a methodology that would affordably help privately-owned businesses around the world with their business challenges and opportunities. I also wanted to provide a resource to help business owners who lack access to good advice and do not know what to do. I envisioned a company that would help business decision makers bring about a new, positive culture in their businesses with energy created by peer advice and coaching. These services would be delivered by experienced and highly trained professionals who embrace my business philosophy and views of life/work balance.

I am proud to say, for the past 25 years The Alternative Board® (TAB) has been doing just that. TAB's peer advisory boards and coaching services have proven to bring about tangible results that cannot be achieved any other way. TAB members are motivated by leveraging the advice from their boards to bring about positive change in their organizations. They are also invigorated by sharing their experiences with other business owners, "paying it forward" to other businesses in their community.

TAB's belief is grounded upon the foundation that business owners need to identify and clarify their personal vision and marry it with their company vision to satisfy the unique picture they have of their future. The TAB system uses an insights-driven approach to help business owners clarify their personal and business visions and identify where change needs to take place. Put simply, TAB helps members to first identify their vision for success and then provides tools, coaching, advice and support to empower members to focus relentlessly and enthusiastically on their vision. They do this because it means something to them, and they do it because their facilitator / coach and board members truly want to see them succeed.

So what exactly is the TAB difference? The key is that we're not doling out theory and platitudes. We provide advice, based on real world experience. The TAB difference involves sharing varying perspectives. While we have found most challenges faced by business owners are common across industries, the insights members gain from members in different industries is invaluable. The results our members receive from their TAB Board makes them better business leaders. The advice is also often life-altering. Being a TAB Board member is a powerful leg-up any business can have over their competition.

Part of the TAB culture is for our members to accept that change is never ending and they must embrace this to get the greatest results, while minimizing the stress that exists in running their businesses. While business owners without a peer support system may fear change, our members are excited and energized by change.

As Founder and Executive Chairman, there is no greater reward than hearing from members around the world about how TAB has helped them with annual sales growth and profits. But more importantly, how they, as a result from being a TAB member, have greater enjoyment in both their work life and home life. They're excited to get back from their TAB Board meetings and implement advice that can help bring about big things for their companies and for themselves personally.

TIMELESS PRINCIPLES OF EXCEPTIONAL BUSINESSES

As we approached our 25th anniversary, we wanted to do something special to share the insights we've learned by working with thousands of businesses over the years. Our mission is to help business owners everywhere improve their businesses and achieve a greater balance in their lives. We, therefore, made the decision to pull together the most important and ageless insights businesses who aspire to lasting greatness should incorporate.

We started this process by speaking with members and facilitator / coaches who have been part of TAB for more than 20 years. We asked them for their insights on how business has changed and the keys to lasting success. We also asked them to peer into a crystal ball and describe how they see business changing in the future. They came up with some pretty amazing insights. One of the overriding insights is that while technology, the business environment and competition continually change, the foundations of a lasting business do not.

We then worked across our community to shape these insights into a set of timeless principles for businesses. Once we had our list, we engaged key experts in our facilitator / coach community on each insight to put together their thoughts on these principles. They shared not only the what, but also why it is important along with some steps that any business can take to start on the path to achieving lasting success.

These 25 articles are the result of this effort. While you may want to read the book cover to cover, my recommendation is to absorb this content slowly. Read one article per week and take time to reflect on the topic. Next, make the commitment to take some tangible action in each area. If all you do is make one single change in each area, at the end of this process, you will find you have made remarkable improvements in your business.

If you find these principles resonate with you, you are energized by the possibility of what your business can become and you want to go further, but you're not sure how, contact us and we can put you in touch with the TAB facilitator / coach in your area. We believe privately-held business owners are the most interesting people in the world. Our facilitators are pretty special as well and would welcome a conversation with you about your business.

I hope you enjoy and benefit from the 25 principles shared in this book.

Allen E. Fishman
Founder and Chairmen, The Alternative Board®
www.TheAlternativeBoard.com

PRINCIPLE ONE

What's Your Red Rose? Differentiating Your Offering

By Ray Brun, TAB Facilitator / Coach,
Oakland, California

I recently heard a story about a woman in Florida who discovered palmetto bugs—which are sort of like cockroaches—crawling out of her drain one morning. She immediately Googled an exterminator who quickly came, got rid of the pests, and left a reasonably priced bill for services rendered.

Unfortunately, the bugs returned a few weeks later, but she couldn't remember the name of the exterminator she used. But it didn't really matter, did it? After all, one exterminator is the same as the next, right? So she searched Google again and called someone else.

The new exterminator came out, sprayed all the drains and left a fair bill for his service. But this time there was one difference. After the exterminator left, the woman discovered a red rose on her countertop alongside a note thanking her for her business.

Should the woman experience another bug problem, do you think she will call the second exterminator? You bet she will. Even more importantly, she will likely tell her friends and family about the red rose she received. She may even write a review online about her experience. In turn, the exterminator will gain new customers directly by referrals from this impressed customer. In business there is no more cost-effective way to acquire a customer than through a referral.

The second exterminator may or may not have been more competent at his job than the first, but he certainly differentiated himself from others in his field. At TAB, the red rose story is a well-known example of why it is important for business owners to find creative, yet meaningful, ways to differentiate themselves and their products from their competitors in the eye of their customer.

THE IMPORTANCE OF DIFFERENTIATION

When you differentiate yourself, people remember you. When they remember you, they spread the word about your business to their network and the world. One cautionary note: A red rose is not a substitute for a great product or service. At its most basic level, any sound business must have a strong product or service offering and it must have talented, committed people working in the organization.

The red rose is an additional twist on the service that makes the business special and memorable. Today's competitive business environment has made differentiation more important than ever, especially with the impact of the Internet.

Tim Alman, owner of Sierra Western Home Loans in Walnut Creek, California and TAB member for 13 years, understands high-touch in a high-tech world. Every day, homeowners mess around with their biggest asset and perform complex transactions while relying on the Internet and phone. However, Tim is a master of the challenging lending process and still makes house calls for all his clients' financial ailments (his red rose).

> *When you differentiate yourself, people remember you. When they remember you, they spread the word about your business to their network and the world.*

Tim asks, "How can you deliver the best solution without genuinely understanding the real purpose of each client's loan and the unique benefits to them for the many options applicable? You must sit at their kitchen table and experience the emotions of both spouses as you learn what they really want, and as you explain their options. Only then can you find their perfect loan."

CREATING A UNIQUE SELLING PROPOSITION

When running any successful business, it's important to clearly differentiate the business in the eyes of potential customers and continually focus on the uniqueness of a company's services or products. This is called a Unique Selling Proposition, or USP, and is the most basic element of every successful company's message. Your "red rose" is encapsulated in your USP.

A well-defined USP constructs a memorable message of these unique qualities and very clearly answers "Why should I do business with you instead of one of your many direct competitors?" Many business owners tie their USP to "good customer service." Unfortunately, there is nothing unique about good customer service, since all of your competitors probably feel they offer good customer service too.

A good product and good customer service are integral to acquiring and retaining your customers. However, a well-written USP defines how your potential customers choose you over a competitor. If you cannot clearly define the uniqueness of your product or service and create some enthusiasm for customers to buy it, you probably don't have the basic foundation for a successful company.

A great example of a familiar USP is, "Fresh, hot pizza delivered in 30 minutes or less. Guaranteed." Dominos significantly changed the pizza delivery market with the implementation of this USP, and they didn't even promise that the pizza would taste good.

My other favorite: "Positively, absolutely, delivered the next morning by 10:30 am." Federal Express literally created the market for overnight document delivery and became so good at delivering on their service that the word FedEx has morphed into our daily lexicon as a generic term for all overnight document deliveries.

One of the fastest ways to go out of business is to attempt to market a product or service that few consumers want, need, or understand. When developing your USP, focus on factors that are most important to the buyers and end users of your product or service—especially the ones that are not easily duplicated by competitors. Be sure to develop adequate marketing assets to communicate your USP, including media advertising, direct mail, internet marketing, packaging and sales personnel.

The simple test of determining whether you've developed an effective USP is whether it sells for you. If it sells your products or services, then you know your USP is meaningfully different.

> *The simple test of determining whether you've developed an effective USP is whether it sells for you. If it sells your products or services, then you know your USP is meaningfully different.*

KEY INSIGHTS

Differentiation of your product or service in the marketplace is important to the long-term success of your business. The business environment is crowded with competition. Having a strong Unique Selling Proposition will help you rise to the top with your target customers. So, what is your red rose?

- Differentiating your product or service has become increasingly important in an ever more competitive business environment.
- Differentiation starts with developing your Unique Selling Proposition (USP).
- Define your USP with a memorable message of your offering's unique qualities.
- The USP must answer the question "Why should I do business with you instead of one of your many direct competitors?"

PRINCIPLE TWO

Don't Just Talk About Company Culture – Live It!

By Rusty Smith, TAB Facilitator / Coach, Houston, Texas

E very company has a culture. It may or may not be the culture the owner would like, but it is there nonetheless. A good analogy for a company culture is the personality of a human being. Someone's personality determines how they communicate with others, how they deal with problems, how they make decisions, and how they process information. Likewise, the culture of a company determines how the members of the organization communicate, both internally and externally, how problems are handled, how decisions are made, and how information is exchanged and processed.

But, what actually determines the culture? In my view, it is based on a shared vision for the company and the shared values of the members of the organization. It is often said that the culture mirrors the personality of the owner, and in many ways this is true... especially for small companies. This makes sense because we tend to hire people who share our values and who buy into our vision. As the organization grows, we hire more people who share our values and our vision and they start to hire people who share their values and their vision, so the culture tends to become ingrained.

> *It is often said that the culture mirrors the personality of the owner, and in many ways this is true...especially for small companies.*

For most companies, this happens naturally. Sometimes, though, things go awry. There is an adage in the management world that, "We hire people for what they know, and fire them for who they are." If we don't have a well-defined hiring process, or we are growing so fast we hire the first warm body who has the right experience or credentials, hiring who is available rather than taking the time to find the right person, we risk hiring someone who doesn't fit the culture. Someone who doesn't share our values and/or vision. If we are lucky, it will become obvious that the person doesn't fit and either we fire them or they quit. If that doesn't happen and they end up hiring someone else who matches their values and their vision, we have begun to slide down a slippery slope.

A better approach is to ensure that the culture of your company isn't left to chance. As the leader, it's up to you to set the tone for the organization by defining the vision and values for the organization. You must live them every day through your interactions and communications with your employees, customers, suppliers and partners. You also need to make sure every employee understands the company's vision and values and they are constantly reinforced. Finally, you need to make sure your hiring process is designed to hire people who fit the culture.

It takes time, but if you want your culture to truly reflect your vision and values, then you have to be willing to put in the effort. If left unattended or unmanaged, the company culture will behave like an untrained dog. If a dog is not trained, it does what it wants, when it wants. Its behavior is unruly and unpredictable and it may attack strangers. However, a well-managed culture, like a well-trained dog, follows the leader, is likely to be well-behaved, somewhat predictable and socially well-adapted.

GETTING STARTED

The first step in defining the culture is to define the vision and desired values. You, as the owner of the company, must articulate a vision for what you want your company to be. *How do you want customers, employees, and partners to think about your company? What niche will you dominate? What word will you "own"? What markets will you be in? What promises will you make to your customers? What measurements (KPIs) are important to you? How will you be different from every other company in the market?* If you can clearly answer these questions, your vision for the company will start to emerge.

To define your values, think of the employees, past or present, you would like to clone. Why would you like to clone them? What is it about them that makes (or made) them the model employees for you? How did they behave? How did they communicate? How did they treat others? How did they solve problems? How did they make decisions? How did they handle company assets? What is common among them? What traits do they all possess? What traits do they all not possess? This is a simple, yet powerful, exercise that you can go through either by yourself, with your TAB Coach, or with your leadership team. A set of descriptors, adjectives, or phrases will start to emerge that will evolve into your "value words" or "value phrases".

JUMPSTART YOUR COMPANY'S CULTURAL EVOLUTION

Consider holding a company meeting where you roll out the new vision and values. For the vision, you need to paint a picture using a lot of visional language. Tell them why it is important for you. Tell them why you think it is important for them. Tell them why it is important for your customers. For each value, have a story that demonstrates that value in action. The stories might be about a customer, an employee, a strategic decision, or anything else that clearly demonstrates how the values came into play. The more stories you can tell, the more people will understand the value. Finally, provide some examples of how you and your employees can implement these values and apply them to processes, such as decision-making and communications. Encourage them to come up with ideas for how the values can be demonstrated.

HOW TO EVOLVE THE CULTURE

The culture isn't going to change overnight. It must be consistently reinforced. The first step is to personally live the culture you create—a responsibility that can be challenging and rewarding when placed in the proper perspective. If you don't walk the walk, no one else will either.

I once heard a story about a young boy obsessed with eating sugar that illustrates living the culture. Despite his mother's pleas and efforts to get him to stop, he refused. Desperate, the mother decided to take him to visit his idol, hoping he could help break the boy of his habit. The mother and son walked for miles in a scorching heat to Gandhi's ashram. When they met the leader the mother said, "My son consumes too much sugar, will you please tell him it's bad for his health?" Gandhi thought about her request and told them to return in two weeks. Although the mother was perplexed that Gandhi didn't immediately admonish the boy's behavior, she did as she was instructed.

> *The first step is to personally live the culture you create—a responsibility that can be challenging and rewarding when placed in the proper perspective. If you don't walk the walk, no one else will either.*

When they returned two weeks later, Gandhi looked directly at the boy and said, "Boy, you should stop eating sugar, it's not good for your health." The boy nodded and said he would do his best to stop. Puzzled, the boy's mother turned to Gandhi and asked why he didn't tell her son to stop eating sugar two weeks ago, to which he smiled and replied, "Two weeks ago I had an obsession with sugar and I needed time to cut back myself."

Another idea to reinforce your values is to make them constantly visible. One TAB member has her company's vision statement stenciled onto the wall of the company lobby so every employee, customer, and supplier sees it when they walk through the door. The values are printed on the back of each employee's security badge. At every meeting, one of the five core values is selected and each employee is asked to share an example as to how they have recently applied that value to their work. Additionally, there is a section for each value on the performance review template, so the employee and the manager can provide examples of when the value was applied or violated.

BIRDS OF A FEATHER

When interviewing potential new team members make sure you discuss your company's vision upfront. Engage candidates in a thoughtful and open discussion about the company's vision by asking for specific examples about how they plan to achieve the stated vision and what will drive their day-to-day priorities. Ask them to tell you a story about how they have demonstrated a particular value in the past.

For example, a TAB member has "company stewardship" as a value. The company has an Employee Stock Ownership Plan (ESOP), so the employees have a financial stake in the company. When interviewing applicants, he asks them to tell him about a situation where they saw a co-worker misuse company resources. How they handled that situation allows him to gauge their ability to handle sticky or difficult situations.

KEY INSIGHTS

Your company culture cannot be left to chance. As a business owner, your vision and values define the culture of your business. Hiring employees that share your vision and live the values in their daily work activities will ensure that your business has a strong culture, and that it is the one that you actually desire.

- A company's culture or "personality" is a reflection of its leader.
- The leader must articulate a compelling vision for the company and ensure that everyone in the organization understands and shares that vision.
- A successful leader lives the values every day and reinforces them in every interaction and communication with employees and customers.

PRINCIPLE THREE

The Moments of Truth:
The Importance of the First 90 Days

BY MARK KOMEN, TAB Facilitator / Coach,
Minneapolis-St. Paul, Minnesota

O n-boarding is a critical factor in establishing successful working relationships with new employees and new clients in any business. The first 90 days set the parameters of the professional relationship over its lifetime. While on-boarding new employees and new customers are two very different business activities, the overall idea is very similar.

ON-BOARDING FOR NEW EMPLOYEES

When looking to add an employee, you've probably met with a number of candidates and have come to understand their backgrounds, perspectives, competencies and work histories. You may have even gotten a sense of their work ethics, personal communication styles and career goals. You've made your decision to hire and extended an offer that the candidate accepted. Now, it's time for them to deliver.

Whether management or staff, your new employee probably had as many, if not more, questions percolating in their mind during the hiring process as you. *Will this be a good fit for me? Will the other staff members accept me? Will I fit in? Will the organization (or owner) help me move towards my professional goals? Do I really have the skills and abilities necessary to perform at the level I was hired for? Will new ideas that I bring to the table about products, markets, customers, or processes be accepted?*

After careful consideration, your new hire decides it's worth the risk. They're coming to work for you and now expectations, on both sides, are high. But truthfully, you're the responsible party; and it's incumbent upon you to lay the groundwork for the future success of your new hire. If you have the following items in place it will help aid in the process.

- A clearly articulated vision and set of core values to let the newcomer know where the organization is headed and what principles are held in high esteem by the owners and staff.
- A clearly defined and supported work culture will establish the behaviors for how things get done and how staff is expected to fit in and succeed.
- A functional and well-deployed strategic plan will facilitate aligning all parts of the organization to achieve its goals and objectives, and allows newcomers to see where their efforts connect to the big picture.

- Well-defined roles and responsibilities, coupled with robust and documented processes and procedures, will help the new staff member get to know the elements of their job, who does what in the organization, where to go with questions, who's relying on them for their work and what their role is in getting things done.
- Effective communication and feedback systems provide staff members with information about what is expected of them and how they're doing.

Steve Gilbertson, a TAB member and owner of a wire harness manufacturer, Electramatic, Inc. in Minneapolis, MN, makes sure new hires have a clear understanding of the company's values, as well as the new employee's job responsibilities. New hires, whether they work on the shop floor or in the office, get a tour of the facility so they can understand how the company operates and what goes into making products for the customer. New hire orientation includes everything from where the lunchroom is located to how to use the computer system. New hires are assigned to a supervisor or lead person in their work area and shadow them for the first few days to learn the nuances of the job. They are also required to take training classes specific to their work assignments.

To make the transition easier, many TAB member companies, including Steve's, hold reviews with their new staff at regular intervals, especially during the first 30-90 days. The point of these reviews is to see how the relationship is going, assess employee performance, and discuss whether up-front expectations are being met. Some members also create specific plans outlining what their new employee needs to accomplish during that first 90-day period, so both parties can gauge their progress.

> *CFO asks CEO: "What happens if we invest in developing our people and they leave us?"*
>
> *CEO: "What happens if we don't and they stay?"*
>
> —Peter Baeklund[1]

ON-BOARDING NEW CUSTOMERS

Now let's turn to the on-boarding of new customers. How much of what we've already discussed applies with regard to attracting new customers to your business? Well, a lot! John Warrillow explains in his book *The Automatic Customer* that the first 90 days of a new customer's experience with a product or service is critically important to the customer's long-term value to the organization[2].

The first 90 days after a new account is opened is an especially sensitive period characterized by several important customer experience factors that include:

- A high level of interaction between the customer and business.
- An exchange of personal information.
- An ability to be flexible and open to new offers or new ideas related to the account.
- A 50-50 likelihood that the customer will defect to another business before fully committing to the product or service.

Customers will also have lots of questions about your business, such as: *Will you deliver as promised, on time? Will you answer my questions and address my concerns in a timely and responsible manner? Will you be in business next year?*

If a new customer experiences the same kind of structured on-boarding process as a new employee and receives tangible value from your product or service in the first 90 days, it will prevent them from having a dreaded feeling of "buyer's remorse."

A New Customer Example

Consider the on-boarding process from your customer's perspective. TAB member Steve Gilbertson brings customers into his plant for a tour and detailed explanation of the process he uses to build their products, allowing the customer to see first-hand what is involved. He also has an extranet on the web where customers can login to review open orders and shipping information. The customer is also able to change pending order requirements, with the information automatically routed to Steve's people for seamless and documented changes. Transparency with customers is the best way to build a solid relationship with them. However, not everyone takes this approach.

A scene from the movie *Tombstone* illustrates the potential for businesses to take their customers for granted:

> Turkey Creek Jack Johnson: "Doc, you oughta be in bed, what the hell you doing this for anyway?"
>
> Doc Holliday: "Wyatt Earp is my friend."
>
> Turkey Creek Jack Johnson: "Hell, I got lots of friends."
>
> Doc Holliday: "I don't.[3]"

Perhaps you, as the business owner, or your staff think, "Hell, we 'got' lots of customers." If a new client feels like they are "just another customer," this is a sure way for them to be a short-term customer.

If you look at the situation from the buyer's perspective, you can see how they may be left with a sense of vulnerability if their first experience isn't exceptional. If each new client feels like they are genuinely valued by the business during the first 90 days, then the relationship will be set on a course that is both long and prosperous.

KEY INSIGHTS

Bringing a new employee or customer into your business has many facets organizational leaders must be skillful in addressing. In the end, it's all about setting, meeting, and managing expectations. The business owner who pays careful attention to the needs of his or her employees and customers will likely develop the most long-lasting and productive relationships.

- The first 90-days are critically important to your customers' and employees' long-term value to your business.
- Have a clear, written business vision and set of core values to share with your employees, clients and potential clients.
- Be able to provide a high level of interaction with new employees and new customers during their first 90-days. This helps develop the relationship and solidifies goals and expectations.
- Make sure your organization is on-track to deliver on promises made to new employees and customers during the first 90-days and beyond.

PRINCIPLE FOUR

Get the Right People in the Right Seats on Your Company Bus (and How It Will Impact Your Business if You Don't)

BY JEAN COOK, TAB Facilitator / Coach,
Tulsa, Oklahoma

We have all heard it before – to succeed, business owners must have "the right people in the right seats." To make that happen, you must have the right people, define the right seats and match the people to the seats. Business owners know this is not easy. But, rest assured, it can be done and it is one of the most important things you can do for your business.

> *"The old adage* people are your most important asset *turns out to be wrong. People are NOT your most important asset. The right people are."*
>
> —Jim Collins, *Good to Great*[1]

RIGHT PEOPLE, RIGHT SEATS AND HOW TO MATCH THEM.

Who are the right people? They are the ones who agree with, and live the company core values.

Your company values must be at the core of how your business is run and how all decisions are made. If you haven't defined your company's set of core values, you must do so, now. Don't hire another employee before having your company values defined. Employees who "get" the values will fit in with the team and they (and their co-workers) will be happier and more productive. Employees who share your values are employees you can trust to make good business decisions, because they are making them based on the company's values.

How to get and keep only the right people? You must hire and retain based on values, not just skill set. To hire the right people, use the company values in your recruiting efforts. Include your values in your job postings to draw the right candidates. Ask questions related to your company's core values during interviews. Don't make the mistake of only asking questions related to the skill or technical aspects of the job during an interview. Instead, include situational questions that provide greater insight into a candidate's values and approach to problem solving.

Retention of existing employees is also driven from your company values. You need to *hire and keep* only the right people. Communicate and refer to your values often. Your employees must know, beyond a shadow of a doubt, what the core values are and how to live by them. Use value scores and comments in your employee review and evaluation forms. It is the responsibility of you and your company leadership to make sure the team knows the values and to coach them on applying the values at work.

Defining the right seats. *Not just an organization chart, but a responsibility ownership definition.*

The temptation here is to use the current organization chart. Do not succumb to this temptation. Organization charts usually reflect the past. You need a fresh look. In defining the seats, look not just at the roles you need for today, but at the seats you need for the future. Look ahead at the company strategy and goals for the next 12+ months and define the roles that will be needed to ensure you achieve those goals.

Companies have three broad kinds of seats – Sales/Marketing, Operations and Administrative. Depending on industry and size of your company, you could have a single or multiple leadership roles for each area. You are defining the roles key to the company's success and the right seat definition must be done independently from thinking about who might fill the seats. Temporarily forget about your current team and define the roles and the key responsibilities under each role. Build out the leadership seats first. Once those are defined you can build out the seats beneath the leadership team.

What makes a good match? *We know what a right person looks like and we have defined the right seats.* Once you have (or are hiring) the right people and you know the seats you need to fill, it is about making that all important match of person to seat. This is about ability. Both the hard/technical skills and the soft/people skills come into play. Define what abilities are needed to meet the responsibilities of each seat and fill that seat with the right person (values match) who has or can quickly get the needed skill set.

Clearly, it takes more effort to find a good fit. But, if your employees are your greatest asset then you should view the effort as one of your best investments. Taking the time to make a good person-to-seat match is much more preferable than the cost of having to replace a bad hire and going through the entire process again.

WHAT HAPPENS IF YOU DON'T HAVE THE RIGHT PEOPLE IN THE RIGHT SEAT?

Wrong Person, Right Seat. This employee has the abilities required to do the job, but doesn't share the company values. He or she is spreading a cancer called dissension: the comment in the hallway, the rolling of the eyes in meetings, the blatant unhappiness that impacts the rest of the team. The result is turnover, a dampening of morale and decreased productivity, all of which are expensive. You know this person must be removed from your company, but they likely won't leave on their own. That means it's up to you. You can't afford to let the cancer spread, so take action to terminate their employment.

Right Person, Wrong Seat. This employee shares the core values of your company but their abilities do not match the requirements of the position. The skill set could be wrong, they might have been promoted (or placed) into a seat "too big" for them. They may have been in the role for some time and outgrown it, making the seat "too small". Although the employee is a "right person," the mismatch will cause malcontent and their performance will be damaged. If there is a right seat for them in your company, move them into it immediately. If that is not possible, you will face the difficult task of having to let a right person go. You should look for the best way to help them to move on from your business into a job that will be a better fit for them. Remember, it is not fair to them to keep them in a job that doesn't fit and you cannot afford the luxury of keeping them just because you like them.

KEY INSIGHTS

Issues surrounding Human Resources are among the most common topics discussed at our TAB meetings. One of our most common and important pieces of advice is to "Hire slow and fire fast". The advice offered by our board members reflects our own – don't hire someone who doesn't fit with your business. If you have an employee who isn't a good fit, don't delay the inevitable: remove the pain.

Take the time to hire the right people and when you have a mismatch take action quickly. Once the fix is in place, everybody wins–the business does better, the other employees' work improves and the leadership can spend time producing results, instead of solving people initiated issues. Even when the fix involves letting someone go, that person will be better off. They have been set free and now have the opportunity to thrive elsewhere.

- It's not enough to have the right people on your team. You also need to have them in the right seat (position).
- Hire and fire based on company values; and reiterate to your employees what those values are.
- Great employees can out-grow their positions in the company. Be prepared to move them into a position that will allow for continued growth and professional development, if possible.
- Employees that are a poor fit will affect the culture, mood, and productivity of the rest of your organization with detrimental (expensive) results.
- No business owner has ever fired too early. If you have an employee that is not a fit with your company values, there is only one solution to resolve that problem.

PRINCIPLE FIVE

If You're the Smartest Person in the Room, Maybe You're In the Wrong Room

By Malcolm Webster, TAB Facilitator / Coach, Vancouver Island, British Columbia

A frican Proverb: *"If you want to go quickly, go alone. If you want to go farther, go together. "*

Years ago, during a graduation address at the University of Texas, Michael Dell, founder of Dell computers, advised graduating seniors to refrain from being "the smartest person in the room." But, if you are, he continued, "I suggest you invite smarter people or find a different room."

One of my great passions is soccer. I recently reminisced with a colleague about a player named Kenny Dalglish, who used to play for the Liverpool Football Club in England during the late 1970s and '80s. Later in his career Dalglish was offered the opportunity to manage the team while still playing and the club continued to experience great success under his leadership. Years later, after he'd retired, Dalglish was asked what the secret to the team's success had been. He simply replied, "I knew I had the team selection right when I couldn't get on it."

As a business owner, you are in the unique position of being both player and manager. You must be involved in the day-to-day operations, applying your energies and passion to serving your customers while ensuring employees remain productive. But in order to safeguard your business you must plan for the long-term and consider what it will take for your company to survive and thrive beyond tomorrow—a process that is, undoubtedly, one of the toughest aspects of operation for many entrepreneurs who don't know when to be on the field and when to stay on the sidelines strategizing.

In 1993, long-time TAB member and owner of Gastineau Log Homes, Lynn Gastineau was at a crossroads with her business. "We had been growing like crazy and I really needed mentoring to get it to the next level." So, she joined a TAB Board to

> *"Decisions don't happen in a vacuum; the best ones rarely come from deep pondering in isolation. They happen when people learn from and draw on the experiences of others."*
>
> —Harvard Business Review,
> *Beyond the Echo Chamber*[1]

provide additional guidance as she worked to move her company forward. It is a decision that Gastineau says paid off because, when you are running a business, "You just don't know what you don't know."

Because Lynn recognized she didn't have all the skills needed to make her business successful and was willing to bring in outside help, she was able to successfully grow her business. However, many entrepreneurs with a viable business plan haven't been as lucky because the owner was reluctant to develop a formalized structure where he or she could obtain objective advice about critical issues related to their business.

The key word here is "formalized." Most business owners talk with family, friends, and colleagues about their business, but avoid establishing an unbiased, and trusted, group of advisors that can provide expertise and relevant information to the entrepreneur when it comes time for him or her to make important business decisions. A formalized process ensures that input from the advisors is taken seriously by the business owner who becomes accountable to his board, to implement any agreed upon changes to the operation. Without the board, it's just another conversation between friends, which is nice, but it won't drive your business forward.

While many large companies have a board of directors, which provides governance in the decision-making process of areas that significantly impact a business, most small business owners decide to forgo an advisory board. Instead, they choose to bear all responsibility themselves, because they believe they don't have the resources to support a board. In reality, they can't afford not to establish a formalized team of advisors who have experience and expertise in all the areas of relevance to their business.

SOME HISTORY

Peer advice is not a new concept. It dates back to ancient Greece, Proverbs ("plans fail for lack of counsel but with many advisors they succeed") and later to Benjamin Franklin's "juntos" (a club for mutual improvement).

In the 1930s, business guru Napoleon Hill is credited with coining the phrase "mastermind." A business mastermind can be defined as a group of like-minded individuals who come together on a regular basis to help and support one another to grow their respective businesses.

When Hill interviewed Andrew Carnegie, inquiring as to the secret of his success, Carnegie replied it could be traced to the "sum total of the minds" of his business associates. He called this combined brain power a "mastermind," and attributed to it the power of his success.

> *"In business, asking questions may not save lives, but it can save you a lot of time and money."*
>
> —Sir Richard Branson

DO GROUPS MAKE BETTER DECISIONS?

Business owner advisory boards work because they ultimately result in the group making better decisions than individuals. Professor Stephan Bainbridge of UCLA School of Law authored a research paper titled "Why a Board? Group Decision

Making in Corporate Governance," which analyzed group decision-making research going back as far as the 1930s. Bainbridge writes "numerous studies have found that group decisions are not only superior to those of the average member, but also to those made by the very best individual decision maker in the group.[2]" There has been a significant amount of research conducted over several decades that points to the effectiveness of the group decision-making process.

In today's world we often feel meetings are not productive and don't result in effective decisions. But a well-managed (facilitated) board of advisors will prove to be an invaluable tool in helping you achieve your vision and goals for your business. It will aid you in being both player and manager of your team with confidence and focused direction.

KEY INSIGHTS

The perfect person who is an expert in all areas of business has yet to be born! The success of your business depends on having a team of people you can talk to when big decisions need to be made, and who can help you prioritize what is really important (versus urgent) and then help ensure you stay on track.

- Accept and identify your weaknesses as a business owner; no one can be the best at everything related to their business.
- Surround yourself with people who are better than you—particularly in areas that are not your strengths.
- A formal board of advisors will be able to provide on-going, unbiased advice on how to take your business to the next level and help you make better decisions.

PRINCIPLE SIX

Are You the Driver of or a Passenger in Your Business?

By Jim Robertson, TAB Facilitator / Coach,
The Woodlands, Texas

"What you get by achieving your goals is not as important
as what you become by achieving your goals."

–Henry David Thoreau

I f you think back to when you first started your business—or
better yet when you first conceived the idea—you may have
had a great vision about what it would mean to you and how
you could fill a need for your customers or community.

The question now is: *Are you realizing those dreams and is your
vision of success being fulfilled?*

One of the most difficult things for any of us to do is look out beyond our immediate horizon and imagine what can be. It's even harder to paint that picture in such vivid detail and bright colors that it becomes a source of daily motivation and constant inspiration.

Most successful people are motivated by their own vision of success. Some make great sacrifices to give the best to their kids, others to buy their first house. We are moved by the stories of ordinary people facing enormous adversity. The common thread among these stories of determination is that people are strongly motivated by the clarity of their vision and purpose.

YOUR BUSINESS GPS

Whether you are a winning sports team, a successful business, or you plan to land on the moon and return the astronauts safely, you share a common thread: having a well-conceived strategy. Any successful business owner will tell you that his or her endeavor was a success because they had a plan they assessed and adjusted as they were building their business.

Unfortunately, too many business owners I have encountered run their business by looking at the past month or quarter results and evaluating whether it was a good one or bad one. This is like driving your car by looking in the rear view mirror. A strategic plan provides a way to start driving your car using GPS and by looking out of the front windshield. The strategic plan is your business GPS. Looking out of the front windshield allows you to adjust to the road and traffic conditions in front of you, rather than the ones you have already passed.

TAB member and business owner, Mark Abels, puts it very well. "Don't just sit back and think the business is going to run itself," he advises. "Put time into your plan. Have a strategy, keep it up, live by it and work to it. Step back and focus on it periodically and at specific times to make sure it's fresh and right."

A robust strategic plan provides not only the path to achieve your long-term vision, but also the framework for making tactical decisions. It will help you answer the following kinds of questions:

- Is hiring a new sales person a key component to achieving my short and long-range goals?
- Will purchasing a new machine sufficiently improve productivity to support my long-range plan?
- Should I spend my time primarily expanding existing accounts or finding new clients?

Every significant decision a business owner makes should be tested against their strategic plan and the tactics they have established to achieve their plan.

Your strategic plan guides you to your goal, helps redirect you when you get off course, and can be revised to respond to changes in your business environment. A good strategic plan is really a very simple document and has three primary components:

- **Where** do you want to end up?
- **When** do you want to end up there?
- **What** the intermediate steps are to reach your goal?

While the resulting plan can be short and simple, crafting the right strategies so that your plan achieves your goal requires analysis, evaluation of alternatives, and selecting the best path forward. Strategy is a vaguely used term in business. As Richard Rumelt explains in *Good Strategy, Bad Strategy,* a strategy involves three specific elements: a diagnosis that defines the challenge, a guiding policy for dealing with the challenge, and a set of coherent actions designed to carry out that policy.

> *As Richard Rumelt explains in Good Strategy, Bad Strategy, a strategy involves three specific elements: a diagnosis that defines the challenge, a guiding policy for dealing with the challenge, and a set of coherent actions designed to carry out that policy.*

Translating your strategic plan to actions and tactics, what you should be doing day-to-day in order to reach your goal, can be more involved. But, it's worth doing. As the adage goes, *"if you don't know where you're going, any road will get you there."*

Operating your business from a strategic plan prevents your business from the dreaded Tyranny of the Urgent. You can spend a little time on the front-end developing a strategic plan that will help you run your business more efficiently to achieve your long-term personal and business goals. Or, you can spend that time in the drudgery of "fighting fires" in the day-to-day trenches of running a business to the ground.

A PLAN FOR THE REST OF US

Many small and medium size business owners cringe at the thought of developing a strategic plan. They find starting strategic planning easy to put off because they manage their businesses by perpetually staying in the "putting-out-fires" mode. We've heard all the common excuses:

- I need to focus on a major company challenge right now.
- I am more "hands-on" than strategic by nature.
- I don't want to be accountable to anyone else.
- My company doesn't have the resources to allocate the time.
- I've tried strategic planning and it didn't work.
- My company is very successful.
- My company is facing tough economic times.

If your vision of a strategic plan is a 4-inch thick binder of useless information that takes months to develop, that's not the kind of plan I'm talking about. You are not General Electric and you do not need to plan like they do. A strategic plan for a privately-owned business needs to be made relatively simple. For example:

> *I intend to be a $5M company in three years. In order to do that I need to finish this year at $1M, next year at $3M and year three at $5M. My key strategies to get there are to develop two new complementary products, increase share of wallet from existing accounts, create differentiated marketing messaging and enter two new industry verticals.*

Congratulations, you have a high level plan!

Now, form your specific action plans and tactics to support the strategic plan and you are well on your way to running a more predictable business. A strategic plan can, and will, help address all the excuses listed above. The direction and clarity that a strategic plan provides will help free-up time, resources and solve major challenges in a proactive – rather than reactive – way.

Key Insights

The difference between successful business owners and those who fail to meet their goals is rooted in how they each spend their time. Successful business owners are forward looking and develop a plan, use their plan to achieve goals and adjust the plan when results or circumstances demand it. Owners who struggle typically operate in a reactionary mode: reacting to customers, employees, cash flow issues, and ultimately decisions regarding the survival of the business. It's your choice. How do you want to operate? How do you want to spend your time?

- Take a moment to consider if your business is allowing you to realize your dreams and vision that you had when you first opened it.
- Whether you are a small or large organization – and whether the business is doing well or not – it is imperative that you develop a strategic plan to achieve your goals.
- Your strategic plan does not need to be a huge, complicated document. Keep it simple by starting with your goal and developing strategies that have a high likelihood of getting you to your goal.
- Include an action plan to accomplish each strategy, which when achieved, will allow you to reach your goal.

PRINCIPLE SEVEN

A Strong Brand Equals Strong Profits

By **Damien Koziol,** TAB Facilitator / Coach,
Basingstoke, United Kingdom

G one are the days when advertisers were able to control the message it delivered to its customers through the traditional mediums of radio, television and newspapers. Increasingly, in today's world, brands are likely to be defined by customer experience and the conversations your customers have about that experience.

Originally, branding was about being able to identify whose cattle belonged to whom—an idea that evolved significantly when, in the 1880s, Coca-Cola was using brand to "differentiate" its cola product from its many competitors. Today, while the outcome of branding is based on differentiation, the way we think about branding has evolved further still. No longer is branding solely about creating a logo. In creating today's brands, marketing directors for a company must also be aware of how services and products are perceived by the public and how much value is gained or lost as a result of that perception.

When managed effectively, consumers attach added value to the product or service, which goes far beyond its physical characteristics and tugs at the heart of an individual's beliefs and feelings, extending our perception of the company itself. Jeff Bezos, founder of Amazon.com, describes branding as "... what people say about (your business) when you're not in the room."

THE VALUE OF A STRONG BRAND

Some people perceive branding as having no tangible value. Yet a closer look at strong brands reveals significant economic value. A simple comparison of assets versus market capitalization will show you that much of the value in a business is perceived. More specifically, products from a strong brand command a higher price. A strong brand is easier to sell. Apple is a great example of the value of a strong brand. At one point, Apple's four percent market share was yielding 52 percent of the profits of the handheld mobile device market, which is more profit than all of its competitors put together.

Branding is also a more efficient way to sell things. A strong brand "pre-sells" a service to a prospect, resulting in a warmer, less skeptical, interaction since most customers are willing to pay for a strong brand.

BRAND EXPERIENCE

The service you offer your customers and the experience they have with you and your business is where consistency and trust are built. This is the most important factor in creating a successful brand. Always keep in mind that what you do matters more than what you say. Strong brands make a promise about the value of the service they can deliver on and one that their customers can believe.

When people's experiences match their expectations, their loyalty increases. The late author and poet Maya Angelou said, "I've learned that people will forget what you said, people will forget what you did, but people will never forget how you made them feel."

> *When people's experiences match their expectations, their loyalty increases. The late author and poet Maya Angelou said, "I've learned that people will forget what you said, people will forget what you did, but people will never forget how you made them feel."*

Anyone can copy what you do—but not they way you do it. It's the little things that matter and every interaction someone has with your product or service is an opportunity to create a positive or negative experience. Period. As the business owner, you and your employees should strive to make each interaction positive and memorable because the best brands deliver a solid product or service, as well as an incredible experience. Muhtar Kent, Chairman and CEO of The Coca-Cola Company, said, "If a brand is a promise then a great brand is a promise kept" and as head of the most iconic brand in the world (with an estimated brand value worth over $80 billion) it is safe to assume he knows something about keeping a brand's promise.

A strong brand does not have to have a remarkable product, although a strong brand cannot be built around a weak product. Sometimes a brand may be built from providing a service that is better than the competition, one people can't help but talk about.

Michael Eisner, former CEO of Disney, defines brand as:

> "...*a living entity – and it is enriched or undermined cumulatively over time, the product of a thousand small gestures. A close examination of great businesses and brands reveal they are mastering the little things. They not only go above and beyond the little things but they put the spotlight on every interaction a customer has with them.*"

BUILDING A STRONG BRAND

The Greek philosopher and scientist Aristotle once said, "If we are what we repeatedly do, excellence, then, is not an act, but a habit."

Applying that logic to brand creation means an entrepreneur must start with clarity and determine what is different about his or her service or product and the way they deliver it to a customer. If you can articulate this difference clearly, at the outset, then you can create consistency in the style and appearance of your brand; the language used to articulate it; and in the experience your customers can expect to receive in every interaction they have with your product, service, or company.

A strong brand is built on consistency. And clarifying your

brand's voice empowers your staff with the tools necessary to deliver a consistent customer experience. This provides the foundation of your *brand promise*. In turn, your staff will become familiar with delivering service that matches the brand you want to portray to your customers.

An important building block in the foundation of your brand will be creating trust between the brand you've designed and the customer you seek to attain. Trust is the ultimate shortcut to a buying decision for a customer. When strong brands consistently deliver a solid service or experience, a customer rewards them by giving the company its repeat business. And if the customer's experience was exceptional, they tell friends and family to try the service or product as well.

Or, as Walt Disney more simply puts it:

"Do what you do so well that they'll want to see it again ... and bring their friends.".

While it might seem that being a successful brand means being all things to all people, the concept is just the opposite. Successful brands target their product or service to a narrow audience and then create a strong connection with them. Targeting your audience enables you to offer your products or services to the customers that have the highest propensity to see the value of your offering and have a positive experience with your brand.

Thom Noller, TAB Member and business owner, learned this lesson first-hand after trying to attract a broad customer market, which was ultimately detrimental to his long-term growth strategy. After a few months in which he lost profits, he decided to refocus on the needs of his core customers. He had found that "If you try to invest the time and money into serving everyone, you'll end up disappointing everyone."

KEY INSIGHTS

Whether you have a plan to build a strong brand for your business, your customers have definitive opinions about the services or products you offer. This means your company has a brand image regardless of whether you've formally created and implemented any specifics. The broader question is: Do your customers have the opinions about your service or product that you want them to have and do they perceive your business in a positive or negative light?

- Consistency and trust are the two most important elements of a strong brand. Make promises to your customers that you can keep and consistently deliver on them.
- Contemporary branding goes beyond creating a logo; it's also about the perception of your products and services in the marketplace.
- A strong brand image adds value to your offering and can command a higher price.
- Don't try to be all things to all people. Identify your target audience and deliver on your promise to them.

PRINCIPLE EIGHT

Stop Working Below Your Pay Grade

By STEVE DAVIES, TAB Facilitator / Coach, Nassau County, New York

T here are three main resources in business: money, people and time. The only one under our control is time. Yet, no matter what you do, it continues to pass. Although there is nothing you can do to stop it, what you can manage is how you spend your time.

It is always easier to do something yourself than have somebody else do it. All too often, business owners wear so many hats in their business they lose sight of the fact a number of the activities they take on are well below the real value of their time. It is too easy to get dragged down by the tyranny of the urgent and lose sight that you are carrying out tasks that should be handled by someone paid considerably less.

When people hear the phrase "time management," it conjures up a picture of lists and methods of prioritizing what you have to do and becomes a tactical exercise amounting to nothing more than organizing activities. That approach ignores the strategic implications of managing **what gets onto those lists in the first place.** It is essential to attack the time management problem at a much earlier stage by taking rigorous control of what you allow into your day. Before you spend any of your valuable time organizing, you must stop working below your pay grade.

This point was driven home by a TAB board member who told me how his partner had decided the value of her time was $450 per hour. A few weeks later, she volunteered to pick up some suppliers from the airport, taking three hours out of her day. When he pointed out that she was "working below her pay grade," she instead booked a car service for $220 and gained valuable time potentially worth $1,350.

The return on that investment works out at over 600 percent, which speaks powerfully to the value of the concept. If you relate to the woman in the story, let me show you how you can stop working below your pay grade.

PUTTING A VALUE ON YOUR TIME

The first step in this process is establishing the value of your time when you are working on the things that bring the greatest value to

Before you spend any of your valuable time organizing, you must stop working below your pay grade.

your business. I call these Platinum Activities, and it is important you take time to identify them properly. They will include areas such as new clients, products, and markets. You should be sure to include all the activities that support your long-term strategic goals.

When you have made a list of your top five Platinum Activities, identify what your time is worth when you are doing them. This number has nothing to do with what you pay yourself and must be calculated based on what value you believe these Platinum Activities bring to the company. I suggest business owners value their time at no less than $450 per hour, and possibly much more.

Once you determine the value of your time, write it down and put it somewhere on your desk where you can see it. Then, use that value as a prism through which you review all the activities that fill your day.

SETTING A TIME GAIN GOAL AND CREATING A TO DON'T LIST

To change the way you spend your time, you need to know not only the value of your time, but also what working below your pay grade is costing you. The best way to give yourself real motivation is to identify how much time you currently spend on Platinum Activities and set a goal for how much additional time you want to spend working on them.

Most people I meet who go through this exercise identify that they spend an alarmingly little amount of time on their Platinum Activities, because they are consumed by the tyranny of the urgent and working on things that are below their pay grade. For most people, there is an opportunity to gain ten hours a week of additional time to work on Platinum Activities. At a $450 per hour rate, that is potentially worth over $200,000 a year.

Most people I meet who go through this exercise identify that they spend an alarmingly little amount of time on their Platinum Activities, because they are consumed by the tyranny of the urgent and working on things that are below their pay grade.

There is a finite amount of time available. To realize your time value gain you have to find those extra hours somewhere. The final step of the process is developing your **"To Don't List."** Every time you find yourself doing something that is below your pay grade, put it on the list. You don't have to take action immediately, but if you write it down and identify what it would cost to have somebody else do it, you will have ample motivation to put together a plan to delegate these tasks and gain the time you need.

MAXIMIZING YOUR PRIME TIME

The final piece is to rearrange your day to handle Platinum Activities during your Prime Time. Each of us has a time in our business day when we are at our peak. Some time management experts recommend doing strategic things in the morning when you are fresh, but plenty of people do their best thinking and work in the evening or even late at night. Identify your best time of day and start to think of this as your Prime Time.

Make a commitment during your Prime Time to work only

on your Platinum Activities. Minimize interruptions during this time, including reading emails and taking phone calls. If you can reorganize your day around Prime Time and turn it into a habit, it will impact your business significantly.

KEY INSIGHTS

Most business owners spend way too much time working below their pay grade. By determining the value of your time and removing activities from your day that are below your pay grade, you will be free to work on things that have a significant impact on your business. It will also give you a language to define what belongs in your day and a technique to identify what to eliminate.

- There are three main resources in business: money, people, and time. Time is the only resource under your control and you can better utilize how you spend your time.
- Create a list of your Platinum Activities–the things that bring the greatest value to your business and identify how much time you currently spend on them.
- Make an assessment of the monetary value of your time when you are working on Platinum Activities.
- Set a goal for the additional hours per week you will spend on Platinum Activities.
- Create a "To Don't List" for those activities that are not important to the value of your business and either delegate, outsource them, or drop them out of your day altogether.
- Identify your Prime Time and reorganize your day so that you can spend this time on Platinum Activities.

PRINCIPLE NINE

I Don't Need An Exit Strategy

By John F. Dini, TAB Facilitator / Coach,
San Antonio, Texas

I don't need to plan an exit strategy. I'm going to run this business until I'm tired and then I'll sell it to some ambitious young person who wants a great opportunity."

In nearly twenty years as a TAB facilitator and coach, I've heard this statement countless times. An entrepreneur starts a business and grows it into a successful entity that he or she can be proud of. It is able to provide financial security for their family, and gains public recognition from other members of the business community, their family and friends, and the community-at-large.

But, as the business owner travels the road to success, he or she forgets to map out a plan for exiting their business and underestimates how unrealistic their expectations may be of a young person taking over. Allow me to dissect the statement above from back to front with some additional analysis.

A Great Opportunity. For whom? Have you taken into consideration the lifestyles of Generation X and Millennials who don't want to work fifty-five hours a week and refuse to be trapped into fixed hours or customer-responsive business models? Your business may not look like a great opportunity to them.

Some Ambitious Young Person. Increasingly, small business ownership is in competition with large corporations for talent. When baby boomers entered the workforce the number of college-educated workers grew six-fold in one generation, and entrepreneurship was the road to success for those who couldn't find a place in a large organization.

But now that retiring baby boomers outnumber those reaching age 45 by four thousand people a day, large corporations are upping the ante for qualified employees. Small businesses will be hard pressed to match a Fortune 500 middle manager's package of a six-figure salary, health care, pension contributions, educational reimbursement, mentoring, and parental leave. Combine those benefits with a defined career path and it's easy to see why an ambitious young person might see a corporate career as the more attractive choice.

I'll Sell It. This is easier said than done. Aside from a shortage of interested buyers, those who may be attracted to small business ownership probably don't have any money. Both Millennials and Generation X are groups that started out in debt and typically remain leveraged throughout their lives. The seller partially or wholly finances most third party sales of businesses with less than $3 million in revenue.

Until I'm Tired Of It. There is a saying among business brokers. When an owner says he or she is burned out, review their

> *Aside from a shortage of interested buyers, those who may be attracted to small business ownership probably don't have any money.*

financial statements. Burnout probably started four or five years earlier, yet it took the owner that same period of time to recognize it. Any buyer wants to see increasing revenues and margins in a prospective acquisition and sellers who are at the end of their rope seldom produce enviable (or saleable) results.

I'll Just Run This Business. This is one of the biggest problems. If you are still running the day-to-day operations of your business, *you* might be the biggest obstacle to a sale. A strong buyer (one with money) wants a business he or she can own, not run. Seasoned management and proven processes demand a premium price. Businesses that are completely dependent on the owner create big discounts in the sale.

I Don't Need to Plan My Exit. Oh, yes you do. And not all exit plans include the sale of the business to an outsider. There are four basic exit strategies that are commonly used:

- Selling or leaving the business to family.
- Selling the business to employees.
- Selling the business to outsiders.
- Closing and walking away from the business.

Even if you intend to simply "close up shop" and walk away from the business, you need to plan for what that will look like for you, your customers, your employees, and your fiduciary responsibilities. How you exit the business needs to align with the

> *A strong buyer (one with money) wants*
> *a business he or she can own, not run.*

long-term vision of your company and your personal life. In order to do that, you need to start planning early for your exit.

A MEMBER STORY

I had a great conversation with long-time TAB member, Eric Aschinger of Aschinger Electric, about his exit plan. He has been working toward the planning and execution of his succession plan for about seven years. From the start, he knew he wanted to pass the business on to the next generation of his family. But, he didn't know if any of them had the desire or leadership skills to take on the responsibility. Eric used personality and intelligence tests to assess the capabilities of his daughters, sons, nephews, and nieces who were interested in possibly taking over ownership.

"I was able to take the results of these assessments, along with other information, to board meetings to get feedback from my fellow board members," Eric recalls. "Using this feedback and bouncing ideas off the board, I was able to make the decision about who would be best to take over, very objectively and confidently." Eric's replacement has been in place as president for several years and now he says, " I'm just helping out and having fun."

Eric did the right thing by starting to plan well in advance so he would have ample time to assess, select, and groom his successor well before he is ready to exit the business. He has a plan for what he wants his exit strategy to look like and has worked diligently to achieve it. Your vision for exiting may look completely different.

Sometimes, the owner really just wants to keep running the business. If it's their personal vision, that's okay. Allen Fishman shares a relevant story in his book *Strategic Business Leadership*. "At a board meeting, Sam Conroy, founder of Conroy Technologies, leaned forward on the board room table during a TAB Board meeting, splayed his hands out as if grabbing the table and said, "Well, I just received an amazing offer – an unsolicited one – to buy out my company." He then mentioned the price, which involved millions of dollars.

Many of his fellow board members eyes widened, thinking, how wonderful this was for Sam. "But," Sam said, leaning back, "I'm not going to take it." One of his fellow TAB members asked him why. Sam Conroy answered, "I know it's an extremely generous offer." He hesitated and then said, "But my business is me and I am my business; there is no separating us." Many of his fellow board members nodded their heads in mutual understanding. For most business owners, their company is one of the most important aspects of their lives and its purpose and emotional value to the business owner is very important.[1]"

PREPARING FOR YOUR EXIT

So, how do you better prepare for the day you will eventually leave? In his book *Finishing Big,* Bo Burlingham identified eight characteristics of business owners who exited successfully:

- Have a crystal clear understanding of who you are, what you want out of your business and why.
- Learn to look at your business as though you are a potential buyer or investor.

- Give yourself plenty of time – measured in years, not months – to prepare for an eventual departure; develop multiple options.
- Have a succession strategy; leave the company in good hands.
- Seek help in the process, not just from exit planning advisors, but also from former owners who have been through the process.
- Consider, carefully, the impact of the sale to employees and investors and gain peace about your decision before moving forward.
- Get a clear understanding of the buyer's motivations so there aren't unpleasant surprises post-sale.
- Have a vision for your life following the sale of your business.[2]

KEY INSIGHTS

It's never too early to begin to plan a strategy for exiting your business. Whether you intend to simply walk away and retire, or structure it to sell at a high profit to an outside buyer, decisions have to be made and implemented. Begin by setting your vision for what you want your post-ownership life to look like and start structuring your business to support that vision.

- As a business owner you need to plan ahead for your eventual exit.
- The market for business sellers is contracting as baby boomers exit entrepreneurial fields. As the labor force shrinks, there is increased competition for the most skilled workers.
- Position your business for sale by reducing the amount of day-to-day operations you handle.
- Prepare for your exit by clearly defining your long-term vision for the company and your personal life, post-ownership.

PRINCIPLE TEN

Why Start with Why?

By David Levesque, TAB Facilitator / Coach, Rochester, New York

W ould you like to find more customers who are indifferent to cost, quality, or convenience? How about
clientele who buy repeatedly from you? What
about customers who voluntarily rave to all their acquaintances
about your product or service? If you answered yes to any of these
questions, get ready to take some notes...

Fred Reichheld, founder of Bain & Company's Loyalty Practice,
is credited with creating the Net Promoter Score® (NPS)[1] – a
management tool that measures the loyalty of customer relationships for a particular business. For the most successful businesses,
profitable, sustainable, organic growth occurs when customers
(and employees) love doing business with a company and sing

its praises to neighbors, friends, and colleagues. Research reveals that a simple survey question can be effective in identifying highly loyal customers who will buy and buy again, regardless of price, quality, or convenience—and actively promote a company's products and services to others.

Let's look at the simplicity of Reichheld's measurement tool, keeping in mind the world is not fair. The following question, which is the NPS question, may be familiar to you. It is showing up on countless company surveys across all industries for good reason.

On a scale of 1 – 10, what is the likelihood that you would recommend our company to a friend or colleague?

Customers who reply with scores from 1 to 6 are considered Detractors; scores from 7 to 8 are Neutral; and scores of 9 and 10 are Promoters. As a business owner, your goal is to have significantly more Promoters than Detractors. Promoters exhibit a loyalty and trust in your products and services that transcend quality, convenience, and even cost—and they'll tell everyone they know just how good you are.

START WITH WHY

A theory as to why Promoters are so loyal can be found in Simon Sinek's book *Start With Why,* which describes the "Golden Circle" and its biological connection to how humans feel, behave, and decide.[2]

Every company knows *What* they do – which is develop and/or distribute the products or services they sell. Some companies can describe *How* they do what they do—the way in which a company delivers its services – in a way that sets it apart from its competitors. But surprisingly, few companies can articulate *Why* they do what they do. The "Why" is a purpose, cause or belief, and provides a clear answer as to why a company exists and why it should matter to anyone else.

Most companies communicate from the outside in: *What* they do and *How* they do it. It's rare that companies communicate *Why* they do it.

The problem with how most companies communicate is that the *What* and *How* do not inspire action. Facts and features make rational sense, but biologically our brains don't actually make decisions based on these characteristics. Starting with *What* is what commodities do. Starting with *Why* is what leaders do. Leaders *inspire.*

Sinek says the correlation to the Golden Circle is grounded in human biology. The neo-cortex was the last part of the human brain to develop. It is the portion of our brain we use for complex thinking and understanding language. The limbic system—which well-preceded the development of the neo-cortex in human evolution—governs how we feel, behave and decide. But it does not support language.

When our *Why* connects with a prospective customer's limbic system it inspires their own feelings and beliefs, creating trust and loyalty based on that trust. The connection to the limbic system inspires behavior and decision making. Those customers (and employees) that identify most closely with our *Why* will give us a score of 9 or 10 on our Net Promoter Score surveys. They are our Promoters. When our communication connects through a prospect or customer's neo-cortex (facts, figures, features, benefits) it may provide a rationalization for supporting a decision, but it's not the same as inspiring behavior or decision-making.

HOW YOU CAN APPLY THIS APPROACH

An elevator speech is a short sound bite (usually 15-30 seconds) that memorably introduces you. Its primary objective is to help you find people who would value knowing more about your company, products, and services. Your elevator speech should be interesting and, perhaps, a bit provocative so the prospective customer or client will ask you for more information. When more information is requested you should then state your Unique Value Proposition (UVP), which is longer–but shorter than 3 minutes. An effective UVP has several parts and will cover the following areas:[3]

- Who am I Story: This tells why you do what you are doing today.
- Who I've Helped Story: This tells how you've successfully helped others with similar challenges.
- Who I Represent Story: This tells why your company does what it does today.

When you express your message as a story (stories resonate with the limbic system, whereas facts and figures target the neocortex), you are addressing and inspiring action and decision-making, which have a higher likelihood of resonating with the listener. Inspiring stories have:

- **A Point.** What are you looking to clarify for the listener?
- **A Setting.** Where the story takes place, an explanation of who the characters are, and the trigger point that sets everything in motion, providing a vital context and interest for the story.
- **Obstacles**. Internal or external challenges that create tension and interest.

- **A Turning Point.** A key decision or action that changes the trajectory of the story.
- **A Resolution.** The wrap-up where you drive home your point and show how everything worked out.

In keeping with the principle of connecting with the limbic system, be mindful that there are six emotions that may come into play when a buyer is deciding to make a purchase.[4]

1. **Fear:** "If I don't make a decision now, I may miss my chance."
2. **Generosity:** "If I make a decision now, I will be helping others."
3. **Greed:** "If I make a decision now, I will be rewarded."
4. **Shame:** "If I don't make a decision now, I'll look foolish."
5. **Pride:** "If I make a decision now, I'll be smart."
6. **Envy:** "If I don't make a decision now, my competition will be better than me."

As you communicate with your customers, keep these emotions in mind as you tell your story. Create an inventory of stories you can select from based on the unique circumstances surrounding your listener's situation and emotional frame of reference. This will allow you to customize and make your "Who I've Helped Story" more relatable to and impactful for your listener.

SOME EXAMPLES

Here are some good examples of why businesses do what they do:

GoldieBlox's aim is to disrupt the pink aisle and inspire the future generation of female engineers.

Uber wants to evolve the way the world moves.

TOM's Shoes believes "We can improve people's lives through business."

Warby Parker believes that buying glasses should be easy and fun. It should leave you feeling happy and good-looking, with money in your pocket.

None of the aforementioned statements tell you what each one does or how they do it. Instead, it tells the why they do what they do, providing the basis for customers who think similarly to connect with the brand.

KEY INSIGHTS

You now have an approach to find your very own marketplace of loyal customers who will not ask you to compete on price. Find your *Why* and communicate it through your Unique Value Proposition. You will find that more and more of your customers become Promoters who are less sensitive to price, quality or convenience; and will actively promote your company to their colleagues.

- Effectively communicating the *Why* of your company will help bring in loyal customers.
- Develop an elevator pitch and Unique Value Proposition that connects to your audience's emotions.
- Connect with your audience on an emotional level by telling a story that connects your business offering to the *Why*.
- Once you've enticed a potential customer with your *Why* you can move on to the 'What' and 'How' of your offer.

PRINCIPLE ELEVEN

Know, Respect, and Leverage Your Competition

BY PHIL YORK, TAB Facilitator / Coach, Chicago, Illinois

T ake a moment to think about your primary competitor. What feelings do they invoke? Do you admire, fear, or loathe them? Your emotional reaction probably depends on whether you are the market leader or a follower. And, if you think you don't have any competition—no matter how comforting a thought this may be—you are fooling yourself. With the pace of technology-based innovation, there are a lot of obsolete businesses out there that wish they had been more observant, humble and innovative.

While many business owners are quick to disparage their

> *Our competitors serve as a great resource*
> *and the best teachers and partners*
> *in an expanding market, while also*
> *providing a benchmark for us to improve*
> *our own services and products.*

competitors, I believe in doing the exact opposite and would advise you to do the same. Our competitors serve as a great resource and the best teachers and partners in an expanding market, while also providing a benchmark for us to improve our own services and products.

Before we dig deeper we must ask ourselves, *What do we gain from competition in general?* First, competitors open and legitimize the market for a business. When there is only one of you in a field, you are, well, a little weird. When there are several, you are normal. Second, competitors standardize the expectations for customer interaction in an industry. This allows a business owner to try new strategies to earn a greater market share. Third, your competitors have interests similar to yours and can influence your industry's business climate, which directly benefits you.

BENEFITING FROM COMPETITION

Competitors serve a dual role of being both an inspiration and a villain. Especially if they are the market leader, they should be looked to as a company to emulate. In the role of the villain, your competitors are a great way to mobilize your employees to achieve more.

You can learn a great deal from your competition. A competitor provides an alternative business model to yours. If you haven't taken the time to study their operating model carefully, you should. What channels do they use? What add-on services do they provide? How do they price their services? There is a lot to be gained from this analysis.

Competitors are also a great source of new product ideas. Sometimes, it is okay to let them lead and then follow fast. Apple has made a fortune out of learning from and improving on competitors that were first in the market. You can also learn from your competitors' business processes. This may simply mean that they have better defined processes than you do. Good processes can be a competitive advantage, so study them closely.

Competitors can also provide you with a great source of potential sales folks and employees, who are trained and proven. Examine their suppliers. Perhaps they are better than some of your suppliers and you should consider a switch.

You can also cautiously view your competition as *coopetition*. That is, cooperators and competitors are all the same. In the role of cooperators, they may be willing to benchmark key processes with you. If you have more to learn from them than they do from you, this is a great opportunity. Also, don't lose site of the fact that buying a competitor is a great way to quickly grow your business. If you're starting to think about your exit, a competitor as a buyer may be a great option.

Finally, competitors are a great place to send your worst customers. Hopefully, you know which customers are profitable and which are not. Give some careful consideration to a clever strategy for directing your worst customers to the competition. It will give the competitor greater bragging rights and you greater profits.

STUDY YOUR COMPETITION

The first step to capitalizing on your competitors is to study them diligently. As the Chinese military strategist and philosopher Sun Tzu wrote, "If you know the enemy and know yourself, you need not fear the result of a hundred battles. If you know yourself but not the enemy, for every victory gained you will also suffer a defeat. If you know neither the enemy nor yourself, you will succumb in every battle." Take the following steps to gain business intelligence about your competition:

- Ask your customers what products they buy from competitors and why.
- Meet with your competitors' vendors and suppliers and learn about their experiences with them.
- Mystery shop your competition. Carefully evaluate them from a client's perspective.
- Interview their employees at trade shows, industry events, and for employment openings within your company.

Most importantly, be honest about your own business. If your competitor has a larger market share than you do, you have a lot to learn from them. Sure, as you study them, you'll find some things that you are better at. Don't take comfort in this. Instead, delve deeply to find those areas where they are better and utilize that knowledge to your advantage.

DEVELOP A COMPETITIVE STRATEGY

Once you develop significant business intelligence on your competition, you need to create a strategy for how you are going to out duel them. "Strategy" is one of the most poorly understood terms in business.

> **Sun Tzu wrote, *"If you know the enemy and know yourself, you need not fear the result of a hundred battles. If you know yourself but not the enemy, for every victory gained you will also suffer a defeat. If you know neither the enemy nor yourself, you will succumb in every battle."***

In his book *Good Strategy/Bad Strategy*, author Richard Rumelt defines a clear treatment of strategy for businesses incorporating three elements: "a diagnosis that defines or explains the nature of the challenge; a guiding-policy for dealing with the challenge; and a set of coherent-actions that are designed to carry out the guiding-policy.[1]"

To illustrate, consider what I believe is the greatest wartime strategy of all time. It was conceived and executed by Hannibal of Carthage in the Second Punic War (218-201 BC). Realizing his country was under threat by Rome, Hannibal went on the offensive and moved his troops into Italy, where they would be safe. The commander then crossed the Pyrenees with his infantry, cavalry, and quite a few elephants.

After the Romans learned of Hannibal's whereabouts they positioned themselves on the opposite banks of the river Trebia where they planned to prevent his advance and destroy him. But Hannibal was a quick thinker. He feigned attack, drew the Romans to his side of the river, and attacked them in front, upon the flank, and in the rear. The Roman army was nearly annihilated and the remaining soldiers fled.

In the case of Hannibal, he diagnosed the strengths of the Roman army, and designed an approach to leverage his army's strengths to take advantage of his enemy's weaknesses. He then developed and executed a set of actions that led to, perhaps, the greatest strategic military success in history.

In the example of Hannibal, it is easy to identify three key aspects of a good strategy—premeditation, the anticipation of others' behavior and the purposeful design of coordinated actions. A strong strategy, as Rumelt explains, is about applying sources of power as leverage to overcome the weaknesses of your competition.

If Sun Tzu and Hannibal were running contemporary businesses, I'd expect they'd be leading their markets. They would know their competition better than the competition knows them, would conceive a well thought out strategy and would execute relentlessly.

KEY INSIGHTS

As a business owner, it is critical that you understand your competition and develop a specific strategy to distinguish yourself and create a competitive advantage. Whatever you do, enjoy the game, learn from your competition, and remain humble.

- How well do you know your competition? You can learn a lot about your business, industry, target market and customers by studying and understanding your competition.
- Learn about your competition by surveying your current customers and prospects, studying your competitor's website and mystery shopping them.
- Keep an open mind. Competitors may provide opportunities for collaboration. In fact, your chief competitor may provide an option to acquire your business or for you to acquire them.
- Once you understand your competition, develop a competitive strategy using Rumelt's three elements of strategy: *a diagnosis that defines or explains the nature of the challenge; a guiding-policy for dealing with the challenge; and a set of coherent-actions that are designed to carry out the guiding-policy.*
- Always remain observant and humble when dealing with your competitors. Don't allow your perception and assumptions to cloud your judgment.

PRINCIPLE TWELVE

Add "Chief Evangelist" to Your Job Description

By Jason Zickerman, The Alternative Board,
CEO, Denver, Colorado

I f you're like me, you probably don't remember many television commercials from thirty years ago. One commercial I don't think I'll ever forget is for the Remington electric shaver. It features entrepreneur Victor Kiam, who famously looks into the TV camera and says, "I liked the shaver so much I bought the company." He then concludes his glowing product endorsement, stating: "It shaves as close as a blade or we'll give you your money back. Guaranteed."

Do you think more men bought those shavers because Kiam owned the company? No question about it. Kiam demonstrated a high degree of passion for his product. He didn't just *say* his product was great. He demonstrated it by going from customer to owner. He also backed it up with a guarantee. Kiam was the Chief Evangelizer for Remington.

Would you buy a product from someone who doesn't actually use their own product? Of course not. A friend of mine works at Coors Brewing Company. The Coors brothers realize the importance of believing in their own products. All employees are required to drink Coors beer and not any other product. Coors employees are well aware of the story of the employee who was fired because he was caught drinking a Budweiser.

The Coors approach may make some people uncomfortable. They may feel employees need freedom of choice to use their employer's product or not. I disagree. As a business owner, you probably disagree too. If your employees are not enthusiastic promoters of your product or service, you need to get new employees.

BECOMING AN EVANGELIST

Do you face the challenge other owners have faced, where they have a good product, but their sales are flat or declining? One common reason for this is you and/or your employees have lost passion for the company's offering. It's not uncommon, if you have been offering a product or service for a very long time, that you may start to get bored and lose the passion for it that you once had. This is especially common for products that don't have a high rate of innovation.

Or, perhaps your confidence has been shaken by a rash of customer defections or poor customer reviews. This kind of feedback causes the owner to sit down and start to wonder if their product or service has lost its edge. There are many reasons why your sales may be lagging. Whether your staff has lost their passion or it is something else, the following steps can uncover the root cause and help you get back into growth mode.

1. Determine your company's Net Promoter Score ® (NPS). You can easily find the details online for assessing your NPS. If your NPS is low or is negative, you have your work cut out for you.

2. Take the time to talk to your raving fan customers, your indifferent customers and customers who have recently defected. Find out from your customers what they like and dislike, and what your product or service might be missing that would fill a need.

3. Do some external market research, particularly if you haven't in a while. Are there new, similar offers that have become competitors or replacements for other competitors? Has your target demographic shifted?

4. Look in the mirror. Have you lost your passion for your offering and is this rubbing off on your employees? If you are no longer the chief evangelist for your product, your employees won't be evangelists either. This will come through loud and clear to potential customers.

5. Assess whether your staff is engaged, energetic and entrepreneurial. If your team is simply "going through the motions," there is no way your business is positioned for growth.

If this process reveals that your employees are not engaged and passionate, one of the most important things an owner can do is to incorporate transparency. TAB Member Michael Benker, of Benker Fire Equipment, explains his approach, "We also have worked to involve key people in the decision making process. By sharing more information about sales and profit margins, they have more of an understanding of what it takes to stay on top, and they will also better understand the reasons for our decisions. For example, the reason why we can't hire more people or purchase new equipment at a particular time is better understood if they know where we are financially."

WHAT IF YOUR PRODUCT OR SERVICE HAS LOST ITS EDGE?

TAB Facilitator / Coach John F. Dini wrote in *Hunting in a Farmer's World*, "If owning your company is a lousy job, the uncomfortable reality is you made it that way.[1]" The same holds true for your product or service. If you don't believe that your product or service is the best offering on the market – if you wouldn't actually use it yourself – then the uncomfortable reality is that this is your doing.

Look, there are a lot of tired products out there. You may have created an incredible product or service 10 or 20 years ago. But, it has not been kept fresh. If your product or service is not fresh enough to excite you and your employees, then you will need

> *If you don't believe that your product or service is the best offering on the market – if you wouldn't actually use it yourself – then the uncomfortable reality is that this is your doing.*

to think about a re-launch. You will want to start with market research to find out what elements of your product or service need to be improved.

KEY INSIGHTS

It is important to your credibility – and to the continued relevancy of your company – that both you and your employees use your product or service. If you're not using your product or service, how can you fully understand the value and areas that need to be improved? More than just using it, you need to be raving fans. As the leader of your company, make sure you add "Chief Evangelizer" to your job description and start by spreading your passion throughout your team. All viable products or services need to be good. But passion is the X-factor that can be the difference maker in whether or not a product or service is successful.

- If you don't believe in the value of your product or service, no one else will either.
- Use your own product or service, and require your team to use it as well, to stay on top of necessary adjustments and connect more closely with your customers.
- If your confidence has taken a hit, take steps to rebound. Identify the source – either internal, external, or both – and develop a plan to turn things around.
- Add "Chief Evangelizer" to your job description and work to spread this evangelization throughout your organization.

PRINCIPLE THIRTEEN

Achieving Business Success through Organizational Alignment

By Blair Koch, TAB Facilitator / Coach, Denver, Colorado

I have worked with many successful business owners and facilitated hundreds of TAB board meetings for over a decade. Yet, it never ceases to amaze me how often the challenges faced by business owners are tied directly to their employees. In short, the goals of the two entities are not organizationally aligned. I have observed business owners that have great products, well-designed processes, and growing companies that struggle mightily with getting the most productivity out of their people.

Throughout this book, my colleagues cover topics ranging from getting the right employees into the right positions based on their skill set, to implementing a strong culture, to the importance of the on-boarding process for new employees. In this chapter, we will look at the structure of organizational alignment in business and provide suggestions for achieving and sustaining it in your own company.

Take a moment to reflect on the following statements. Ask yourself if you're able to answer "yes" to each one.

- I have established a written company vision and I have communicated it clearly to my employees.
- Employees in management understand my vision, and the goals that I have set forth, and are leading their teams in a direction that ensures that we will achieve our company goals and objectives.
- Our company effectively motivates employees to achieve goals.
- Most people who work here feel fulfilled.
- Internal procedures are clearly communicated in writing and employees are fully aware of what is expected of them in their positions with the company.

Now, put yourself in the shoes of your management team. Consider the following questions from their perspective:

- Do you consistently bring a high degree of value to the company?
- Right now, would you say you are satisfied with the impact you have on your organization?
- Are you using your abilities to the maximum potential on behalf of your company?
- Would you say that, on a typical day, there is universal clarity about critical work priorities?

If you believe each of your managers would answer YES to the questions, congratulations! You have achieved an aligned organization.

Usually, when we ask management teams the alignment questions, in private, their answers vary between uncertainty, hesitation and a firm "NO". They tend to think that they bring some value to the organization, but they wish they could do more and have a greater impact. They do not feel they are using their abilities to the absolute fullest.

A lack of alignment between a business owner and his or her managers and employees can keep a company from reaching its maximum potential. In extreme cases, it may destroy the business if the employees are consistently out of step with the vision and goals established by the owner.

> *Alignment is the side-by-side effective working relationship in an organization that generates great results.*

CHALLENGES ACHIEVING ALIGNMENT

Anyone who runs a business knows that trying to get everyone on the same page in an organization with any regularity is like trying to coax a six-ton elephant into a Volkswagen Beetle. So, it should come as no surprise that many business owners have never been able to achieve organizational alignment in their business.

Lack of alignment is no one's fault. The owner believes he or she has made the company vision, critical success factors and goals crystal clear. Nearly every employee is trying to do a good job and play a significant role in making the company successful. Yet, in most businesses something breaks down along the way and what the owner is trying to achieve is misaligned with what the organization is doing.

A great deal of time is wasted in non-aligned companies. Why? Because people are working on the wrong priorities, wasting time on things that are not essential to the success of the company, or duplicating tasks that other people are already working on. It's a downward performance cycle. *That cycle only turns around when you make a commitment to alignment.*

THERE IS A BETTER WAY

The good news is that a lack of organizational alignment does not have to be a way of life for you or your business. The key to an aligned organization is that the owner and management team members have a harmonious, constructive business relationship, and are working 100% toward common goals. Ask yourself:

- Would you like to be able to accomplish more each week, using the same number of working hours? Would you like the whole management team to be able to do that? Aligned organizations are crystal clear on roles and priorities and are able to achieve more.

- How many times have you found people in your company working on something they weren't supposed to be? Or working on something somebody else was already working on? Aligned organizations have common priorities that everyone is working on. A high degree of communication prevents working on the wrong or duplicate activities.

- How much longer do you want that pattern to continue?

Your business really falls into one of two categories—it is either moving closer to alignment with the owner's vision, or moving away from alignment.

BECOMING AN ALIGNED ORGANIZATION

Alignment challenges usually come down to relationships issues between the owner and the management team. An alignment issue reflects two sides of the same coin. Neither the owner, nor the managers can improve alignment on their own. However, if both parties are willing to engage, you can transform these relationships for the better.

There are two keys to improving alignment:

1. The first is the owner's commitment to the process, which is absolutely essential.
2. The second is the management team's willingness and ability to tactfully, but assertively, engage for constructive change.

Once the commitment is made by both parties, the necessary breakthrough can occur using the following best practices:

- Create a communication environment where employees are encouraged to contribute ideas and provide constructive feedback. Effective communication goes both ways. Employees need to accept that their input will be considered, but not always accepted.
- Establish a written company vision statement that aligns with your personal vision. Communicate this widely with all employees and reinforce it in daily activities.
- Engage with the management team to clarify company values and establish the culture which is the embodiment

of those values. Do not tolerate employees who do not fully buy into your values and culture.

- Work with the management team to conduct an honest SWOT (Strengths, Weaknesses, Opportunities, Threats) analysis of the business.
- Develop an organization chart that outlines the specific responsibilities for each role. This process will eliminate any overlap in tasks and responsibilities.
- Create documented critical success factors, strategic plans and prioritized actions that have buy-in from the management team.
- Establish weekly meetings to track progress, resolve issues and adjust plans.
- Periodically turn the wheel. That is, take the time to step back and assess whether the current strategic plan is still the best one and whether you continue to be fully aligned with the management team.

KEY INSIGHTS

Alignment is more than a way of working with your key staff. It is a way of life. Alignment starts with commitment – from the owner and the management team. When both the owner and the management team commit to improving organizational alignment, the organization will achieve measurably better business results—and the business experience will be considerably more enjoyable for you and your staff.

- Make an honest assessment of your organization and especially whether your relationship with your management team is functioning as well as possible.
- If your assessment reveals room for improvement, make a commitment to improving organizational alignment.
- Begin a dialogue with your management team on ways in which you can work together more effectively to improve trust and create a respectful working relationship.
- Commit to following a structured process to transform the communication, culture and collaboration of your organization – starting with your management team and extending throughout your organization.

PRINCIPLE FOURTEEN

Business Yoga: Flexibility as a State of Mind and Practice

By KATIE FRITCHEN, The Alternative Board,
Marketing Manager, Denver, Colorado

A tree that is unbending is easily broken.
—Chinese Proverb, Tao Te Ching

When most of us in the western hemisphere think about the word *yoga* we associate it with Hatha yoga, consisting of a series of poses such as downward dog, warrior, tree, etc. The practice of yoga, however, is really so much more. It includes the practice of separating from your lower self – your ego – in order to attain a state of higher consciousness and self-awareness. When practicing yoga, you're not simply moving through poses, but using physical exertion to enhance mindful intention.

During a recent class (yes, my mind did wander to work–don't tell my instructor!), it occurred to me that yogic practice, both the physical and mental aspects, translates perfectly to business flexibility. Let me explain further.

My yoga instructor begins each class with a short meditation to clear our minds and set an intention for our practice. It is in this moment of intention that one's path to enlightenment begins. Because if you're not practicing with intention, you're simply going through the motions.

Similarly, if you did not start your business with intention then you're working on someone else's dream or you're self-employed (or both). When you define the intention of your business—and this applies to your personal life, too—then your company has purpose. Purpose is what will help you to move your operations fluidly in a changing marketplace, laying the groundwork for a strategic, but flexible, plan.

OPERATING AT A FRENETIC PACE

We live in a fast-paced world where advances in technology and globalization cause a whirlwind of change in market conditions. This pace may impede our decisions related to business operations as we work to keep our company relevant in the marketplace.

At this pace, it is easy to think of business flexibility and strategic planning as two elements of business that are at odds, when in fact they are complimentary. When used in tandem in your business they can provide a competitive advantage in a dynamic marketplace as you work to develop long-term strategic goals.

While it's true smaller start-ups excel at being able to pivot with these changes, attributable, by most analysts to having a small staff, a flat organizational structure and a focus on nurturing an innovative culture, you don't have to be a small start-up to be successful in being flexible in your organization. You do, however, need to make the commitment to thinking differently and developing a company model that allows for a flexible business structure. Ultimately, it is you who will make the decision to either break under your own rigidity or find new movement in the flow.

LET'S MAKE IT MORE CONCRETE

To illustrate how flexibility and strategic planning work together, let's take a look at the teaching of Lama Surya Das, one of the most highly trained American lamas, or spiritual leaders, in the Tibetan Buddhist tradition. Das describes "The Six R's of Intentional Responsiveness"—a concept of allowing space for consciousness to guide you in your decision-making, rather than emotional reaction—in his book *Make Me One with Everything: Buddhist Meditations to Awaken from the Illusion of Separation*.[1]

Das describes "The Six R's of Intentional Responsiveness" as an anger management technique, but I believe it can be just as impactful in business as well.

1. RECOGNIZE

The first R is to recognize the cause of the need for change. This may seem like the simplest of the responses, but in reality it can be the toughest. For one thing, your *asmita* – the aspect of ego that is the three-year-old child in your head saying, "Mine. Mine." – can cloud your ability to recognize some change or redirection is needed. I guarantee if you have the "This is my business and we'll do it my way" mentality, you are limiting your ability to effectively recognize, and apply change, to your company's environment.

2. RECOLLECT

The sooner you recognize the need to make an adjustment, no matter how big or small, the easier it will be for you to move to action. If you move to action too quickly, then you have reacted, instead of mindfully acted. Yogis suggest practitioners take the time to pause and mindfully recollect on past experiences, reactions, and results. While it need not dictate our present and future, factoring recollection into course correction will result in a more thoughtful response.

3. REFRAME

This refers to the act of "stepping back" and observing a challenge from a different point of view and is another yogic teaching that has direct implications in the business world. Make sure you are looking at each new change from the perspective of your stakeholders, which include your customers, employees, target market, community, and competitors.

This is an area where the organizational structure and culture of your business will come into play. For example: *Have you created an internal environment where your team feels comfortable presenting new ideas? Are those ideas heard and authentically considered? Is your asmita – your ego – limiting your company's ability to innovate? Is your company so stuck on the traditional tiered organizational structure that you are overlooking the skills and perspectives of younger, less experienced, and new talent in your company?*

As you approach this step it can often reveal truths that are not particularly flattering. It's better to face the truth and work to improve the future, rather than be blissfully running a flawed organization.

4. RELINQUISH

Yogic practice teaches us to accept the natural feelings that arise in all of us and then let go of those feelings. It helps us let go of those thoughts and feelings that are counterproductive. Instead, as the practitioner, you are encouraged to seek to understand your feelings, which is a bit more conceptual than the previous three Rs, yet still relevant to business flexibility. Remember, change can be scary and exciting, overwhelming and enlightening. But if you embrace these emotions as part of the process to become a truly flexible organization, genuine insight is possible.

5. RECONDITION

Reconditioning your intention is also a bit conceptual, but a very important step in responsiveness. In this step you are reconditioning your own thoughts and behaviors to purge your business decisions of those emotional reactions that don't serve you. Part of the process involves allowing yourself the time and mental space to step back from the day-to-day needs of running your business and making decisions as a business owner. Reconditioning will help you mindfully dismiss unproductive actions by replacing them with intentional responsiveness.

6. RESPOND

You now have the information and mindfulness necessary to respond to changing market conditions proactively and with intention. Sometimes your response is to simply do nothing, other times it will be to take drastic action. No matter the level of response required, by working through The Six Rs of Intentional Responsiveness with purpose, you can be confident knowing your response will be aligned with your goals, and not reactionary.

FLEXIBILITY ENABLES PIVOTING

Perhaps you are wondering "Why do this? It looks like a lot of work." Flexibility enables you to make a pivot in your business. Entrepreneur guru Eric Ries has written extensively about the importance of business owners being able to pivot in *The Lean Startup*. Ries explains that being nimble enough to pivot is critical to the success of both start-ups as well as to innovators in established companies.

Ries writes *"Famous pivot stories are often failures but you don't need to fail before you pivot. All a pivot is, is **a change in strategy without a change in vision**. Whenever entrepreneurs see a new way to achieve their vision–a way to be more successful–they have to remain nimble enough to take it.²"*

> *Ries writes "Famous pivot stories are often failures but you don't need to fail before you pivot. All a pivot is, is a change in strategy without a change in vision. Whenever entrepreneurs see a new way to achieve their vision–a way to be more successful–they have to remain nimble enough to take it.²"*

KEY INSIGHTS

Confidence in your vision and strategy is good. Complementing your confidence with flexibility is even better. With a little practice, application, and discipline you will notice you are more comfortable with being flexible in your decision making process. By practicing intentional responsiveness, you will awaken the ability to move with fluidity in your business environment while maintaining your long-term strategic vision.

- Flexibility in your business is required in today's changing business environment.
- Navigate change with purpose and intention by having a strategic plan to refer to when making business decisions.
- Use The Six R's developed by Lama Surya Das to help reduce reactionary decision-making: recognize, recollect, reframe, relinquish, recondition, and respond.

PRINCIPLE FIFTEEN

Lifelong Learning: The Ticket to Business Success and a More Fulfilled Life

By David Halpern, TAB Facilitator / Coach,
Denver, Colorado

Adaptability is crucial not only for survival in the wild, but also for survival in the business world. Any business owner who wants to succeed and grow their company must be able to adapt to change. However, before adapting to change you need to see the change coming.

"I skate where the puck is going to be, not where it has been," said hockey great Wayne Gretzky. The quote was a favorite of the late Steve Jobs, founder of Apple, who believed it represents the competitive advantage that his company has always brought to its innovative products.

Jobs took great pride on being attuned to industry, technology, and consumer trends that his company and team applied to the design, marketing and selling of its products. Essentially, his company bet on where the "puck" was going to be in the future and then arrived at the goal with a solution to satisfy the needs of their customers.

Jobs also attributed his company's success to openness. "A lot of people in our industry haven't had very diverse experiences. So they don't have enough dots to connect, and they end up with very linear solutions without a broad perspective on the problem. The broader one's understanding of the human experience, the better design we will have."

Adaptability and perspective require a willingness to explore outside one's known universe while seeking out and absorbing knowledge from a variety of sources, and then employing that knowledge in service of your business strategy. The most successful people in business are lifelong learners. If you want to be successful in your industry, join the lifelong learners club and you may find yourself sitting among the top entrepreneurs in your field.

Lifelong learning is a commitment by an individual to continue to increase their knowledge base, perspective and self-awareness throughout their lifetime. For individuals where the status quo is never good enough, lifelong learning satisfies the desire they have to be better informed and to have a broader perspective.

> *Lifelong learning is a commitment by an individual to continue to increase their knowledge base, perspective and self-awareness throughout their lifetime.*

Lifelong learning can be achieved in different ways. Some lifelong learners increase their knowledge through books and formal classroom training. Other lifelong learners are curious individuals who increase their knowledge through insightful questions and invigorating conversations with other people. Some learn by teaching and others by doing. Regardless of the method, lifelong learners tend to be interesting individuals who are continually seeking ways of filling knowledge gaps and doing things differently.

WHY ASPIRE TO LIFELONG LEARNING?

"Education is not the filling of a pail, but the lighting of a fire." – William Butler Yeats

Lifelong learners are motivated to learn and develop because they view the acquisition of knowledge and skills as a deliberate and voluntary act that enhances our understanding of the world around us while providing us with more and better opportunities to improve our quality of life.

For example, lifelong learning keeps your brain healthy. Henry Ford said, "Anyone who stops learning is old, whether at twenty or eighty. Anyone who keeps learning stays young. The greatest thing in life is to keep your mind young." Ford's assertion is backed by a number of scientific studies that link learning to brain health, improved memory, and reduced incidence of disorders such as dementia and Alzheimer's.

From a business perspective, lifelong learning makes you a better leader because when you expand your horizons it enables you to meet people where they are, resulting in better relationships between you and them. Your willingness to learn new things and be open will also support your relationships with employees and provide you greater influence in your business partnerships and negotiations.

The greater your knowledge base, the bigger the stockpile of solutions you have at your disposal to tackle problems and overcome challenges. When you learn about subjects outside your area of expertise, you reduce the temptation of getting stuck in thinking or doing things that are one-sided. You also increase your ability to problem solve because learning something new often requires the same skills—persistence, creativity, and humility.

You may also find that lifelong learning brings you greater self-fulfillment. There is a pride associated with learning a new language, mastering a new skill, or exploring a new world you were previously unfamiliar with. Additionally, embarking on new learning adventures can lead to opportunities that enrich your life, such as meeting others with similar interests and an expansion of your social circle.

For all these reasons, lifelong learners have a great advantage in business and tend to lead more fulfilling lives.

How to Become a Lifelong Learner

So how do you cultivate the habit of lifelong learning? Here are a few tips to get you started.

- **Establish goals.** What do you want to learn? Each year, set aside time to set goals regarding specific skills and knowledge you want to acquire.
- **Find your sources.** After you establish your learning goals take some time to gather your sources.
- **Find a group.** While many of your learning goals can be pursued alone, sometimes it helps to have a group of people to learn along with you.
- **Ask questions.** Effective learning requires active participation. You can't passively consume information. As you

read and gather your information seek to engage experts in that area.

- **Be vulnerable.** Sometimes, business owners trap themselves. They may feel the need to be the smartest person in the room—especially in the presence of employees, suppliers and customers. This is a mistake that keeps you trapped by what you already know. In today's world, the inner-workings of business are more transparent and the people doing business are more authentic. It's okay *not* to have all the answers or knowledge. When you are open to learning from employees, customers, and vendors it helps you fill your knowledge base.

- **Learn from your employees.** If there is something they can teach you, don't hesitate to ask. For example, if you want to learn more about social media then assemble all of your employees under 30 once a week and pick their brains on the subject. You will quickly become very educated on the subject and your employees will feel good about helping you and sharing their knowledge.

- **Practice, practice, practice.** Don't just read or listen your way to knowledge. Find a way to put that knowledge to work. As Benjamin Franklin wrote, "Tell me and I forget. Teach me and I remember. Involve me and I learn."

KEY INSIGHTS

Before adapting to change you need to see the change coming, which means anticipating where the puck is going to be. Lifelong learners have a great advantage in this area and tend to lead more fulfilling lives. President John F. Kennedy said, "Leadership and learning are indispensable to each other."

- Lifelong learning is the pursuit of continued educational experiences to fully engage the brain, heighten physical activity, and maintain healthy social relationships.
- Become a lifelong learner by establishing goals, finding sources, and asking questions.
- Don't stay trapped in what you already know. Be open to learning from your peers, employees, customers and vendors.
- Don't just learn—implement and do!

PRINCIPLE SIXTEEN

A Little More Life and a Little Less Work: Achieving a Work-life Balance

BY DAVE SCAROLA, The Alternative Board,
Vice President, Denver, Colorado

Many entrepreneurs chose to be business owners so they could retain more control over their lives, only to find that instead of controlling their business or their lives, their business is actually controlling them.

There's nothing more exciting than breaking free of cubicle life and starting your own business, where you can be your own boss and make your own rules. You get to decide how to spend your time, who you want to surround yourself with and what the priorities are. The benefits to running your own company are, indeed, plentiful, but not without compromise.

One drawback of entrepreneurship is having no safety net–you're putting most, if not all, of your eggs in the basket labeled, "I'm going to start a business and it's going to be a success." Other drawbacks are stressful decisions to be made on a regular basis regarding hiring, firing, pricing, planning, partnerships, and more. As these stresses begin to pile on, the work-life balance scale tends to tilt toward the work side, and in some cases, crashes to the floor.

We decided to sort fact from fiction of what the work-life balance structure of a small business owner looks like by surveying hundreds of business owners. Here is a brief snapshot of what we found:

- 49 percent work at least 50 hours and 19 percent work 60-plus hours.
- 79 percent believe they are working too hard.
- 56 percent would like to work less than 40 hours.
- 93 percent of owners sometimes work on weekends, with 40 percent working always or often.
- 56 percent of owners take 15 vacation days or less while 32 percent take 10 days or less.
- 76 percent report feeling work-related stress in the form of impatience, insomnia and forgetfulness.

Achieving a work-life balance means a balance between your work and everything else important in your life. Your business model should allow you to spend time on the non-business areas of your life that give you true fulfillment. Some newer business owners try to morph work-life balance into their business by creating a family-like culture in their business, thinking this will give them fulfillment. This is good to aspire to, but they often find this is not enough. If you haven't designed your business in a way to enable your personal interests, then you've really just created a job for yourself.

> *If you haven't designed your business in a way to enable your personal interests, then you've really just created a job for yourself.*

WHY IT'S IMPORTANT

I have found some business owners downplay the importance of using their business to enable their desired lifestyle. Some of them feel they will be judged by their peers, colleagues and even employees, if they use their business to achieve the lifestyle they aspire to. The personal vision of each owner is different. Some want to live like royalty and others just want to spend more time with their spouse, children or grandkids. As the person who took the risk to start the business and has to make all the difficult decisions, you should embrace your business as the vehicle to achieving your desired lifestyle.

The reality is the lifestyle you create has a great deal to do with your personal energy and effectiveness as the leader of your business. If your lifestyle is not providing the time needed to recharge your emotional and intellectual batteries, you will not be able to create the energy output required to attain and sustain success in your business.

HOW TO ACHIEVE IT

Just as you have a plan for your business, you need to design a plan for your lifestyle outside of work. Many people feel their lifestyle isn't what they would like it to be, not recognizing it is only because they have not taken the steps to define or create one that would satisfy them. For example: *How many days of vacation would you like each year? What time do you want to arrive at and leave your office each day? Do you want a second home on the lake?*

Once you have listed or mapped out your aspirations, you need to define the changes that need to be made in your business to support them. For example, you may need to delegate tasks and responsibilities to others in your business, so that you'll have more time to enjoy life outside of your business. Or, you may need to make the commitment that you are going to take Friday afternoons off.

WORK-LIFE BALANCE IS NOT FOR EVERYONE

As a society that has always been known more for its productivity and less for its leisure, it may surprise you to learn that not everyone aspires to creating a work-life balance in their lives. Many business owners gain the greatest fulfillment in their lives from being very hands-on owners.

Sean Baker, founder of Baker Fabrication, is a prime example of someone who remains involved in his business. When the octogenarian was asked why he still works so hard, especially given the fact that he's financially secure, he said, "It's not about the money. I do it because I live it and love it. I go to bed at night thinking about my current and future projects and **get up in the morning with a purpose.**[1]"

"It's not about the money. I do it because I live it and love it. I go to bed at night thinking about my current and future projects and get up in the morning with a purpose."

WITH STRATEGIC PLANNING, WORK-LIFE BALANCE FOR ENTREPRENEURS IS POSSIBLE

Some clear trends emerged from our work-life balance survey, such as the desire to spend more time with friends and family, a belief by many that they are overworked, and a desire to work less than forty hours a week. But, we were also pleasantly surprised to find how truly eclectic and diverse our entrepreneurs revealed themselves to be. For example, there are plenty of owners who have figured out how to successfully run a business while working less than 40 hours a week. It's heartening to know that balance is possible.

As a business owner, you will always be faced with the challenge of trying to achieve a healthy work-life balance, because entrepreneurship comes with a list of inherent risks and responsibilities. If it was easy, everyone would do it. But, if you are able to align the strategic plan of your business in a way that supports your lifestyle, your stress will be reduced and you will be able to achieve more balance in your life.

KEY INSIGHTS

You started your business for a reason and chances are it was not so you could work 60-plus hours per week. While most business owners struggle to achieve a work-life balance, you can avoid this trap by identifying your lifestyle goals and creating a plan to achieve them by choosing to tip the scale back to its center and start living a life that is free from many of the day-to-day tasks of running your business.

- Achieving a work-life balance requires the same thought, effort and focus as creating and building a business.
- Take some time to sit down and write down your lifestyle goals that focus on your life outside of your business.
- Create a plan that includes delegating some of your daily work tasks to other employees.
- Review the strategic plan for your business with an eye towards whether it will support your lifestyle or personal vision. If not, make the necessary adjustments to better align your personal and company vision of success.

PRINCIPLE SEVENTEEN

The 90-Day Challenge: Have Your Business Run Without You

BY JEFF WHITTLE, TAB Facilitator / Coach,
Dallas, Texas

C lose your eyes and imagine you've left your business for an extended vacation— a *real* vacation. You've vowed not to read email. There will be no scheduling of daily status updates or phone calls. You will completely disconnect from the business you've built, allowing it to run without you as you sit back and finally enjoy the benefits of being your own boss. No contact, no meddling, no worries.

If you're like many business owners, you've probably broken out in hives just thinking about what could happen to your business if you actually unplugged for an extended period of time.

We've all heard the adage, "You have to build a business that can run without you." Truth is, precious few business owners actually pull that off. Instead, most stay firmly planted in the tactical minutia that can suck the life out of them and the hours from their days, as opposed to building businesses that run without them. They've constructed a company in which each spoke of the operation must connect to them, otherwise everything will fall apart.

> *We've all heard the adage, "You have to build a business that can run without you." Truth is, precious few business owners actually pull that off.*

This, of course, is a pity because we started our businesses looking for more than that. We had a passion, a mission, and things we wanted to accomplish in our lives. We believed entrepreneurship would free us from the constraints of traditional employment so we could actually do those things we enjoy most. Rather than punching clocks, we would be our own bosses and our business would set us free. But, instead of freeing us it often feels like we're imprisoned by them. Do you know why?

Because, most of us simply won't let go. We clutch desperately to the false comfort of making every decision or approving every potential deal. We rationalize, "How can I possibly count on someone else to do the important work? They might screw it up." We surrender to the fear an employee might make a mistake that we wouldn't have made.

We treat our businesses like nervous parents who convince themselves they're teaching their child to ride a bicycle. But, in our case, we're never quite willing to remove the training wheels.

The result? Most owners have created a business doomed to wobble along, forever held back by the friction of the training wheels they refuse to remove. The irony is when you build a business that you won't let go of, you've built a business that won't let go of you.

Thomas Edison said, "If people would do what they are capable of they would astound themselves." The correlation for TAB is if business owners would allow their employees to do what they are capable of, the business owner would be astounded.

The advice from one TAB member on this subject is spot on. He advises to, "First, surround yourself with good people and then get out of their way. We all hire adults, let them make decisions and don't be afraid to delegate."

As business owners, we spend so much time working in our businesses that we don't give ourselves the time to step back and really enjoy life. Business ownership is so much more than the technical skills needed to perform a job. Owners often adopt this mindset because they are good at the thing that started the businesses – for example, they are a good technician – so therefore they believe they are also immensely qualified to run all aspects of the business. Once you become a business owner, you're also in

> *The irony is when you build a business that you won't let go of, you've built a business that won't let go of you.*

the business of running a business. You're not going to have all the answers, and that's fine. The key is to recognize your weaknesses and either improve on them or hire someone who is strong in the areas in which you are not.

THE 90-DAY CHALLENGE

One way I've seen business owners break out of this doom loop is by agreeing to take a 90-Day Challenge where they challenge themselves to think differently about all aspects of their business. They question what they think they know about it. They challenge their assumptions and the processes with regard to "the way we do things," which can sometimes limit the true potential of their businesses, borne by a false sense of security through familiarity and what they know is safe.

For 90 days, I encourage owners to get outside of their comfort zones and delegate to others many of the responsibilities they've tightly clung to over the years. By challenging themselves to use this model, they begin to think about their business differently and establish clearer strategic goals, while learning to chart a course, delegate responsibility and take the first steps toward running their businesses.

And guess what? They like it.

Business owner and TAB member, Ben Allen had a dream to take an extended volunteer trip with his family to Tanzania. But, he was so stuck in his business that he didn't think it would ever be possible. Ben recognized he didn't have the skills to structure his business to run without him, so he made the decision to hire a business manager. For eighteen months, they worked together to identify the right employees and empower them with the responsibilities that Ben had shouldered himself. Because Ben was able to step back and delegate more of the responsibilities in his business, he and his family were able to realize their dream and spend seven months in Tanzania helping to build schools.

The key to Ben's success was three-fold. First, he identified, trained, and empowered employees who would take on the work needed to keep the business running while he was away. Second, he and his business manager created a state-of-the-art documentation system for all the procedures and processes needed to carry out the work. (The system was built so that new people could come in and have everything they needed to start working from day one.) Third, and perhaps the most difficult, he let go. Ben had to let go of the "my way or the highway" mentality that many business owners are stuck in and allow his team to make big decisions without him.

While Ben was away, his company posted the largest profit month in its history. Additionally, clients raved about the huge improvement in customer service. When Ben returned from his overseas trip, he found himself faced with an entirely changed company. The company had purchased an office location and moved the team from being remote into the office, and hired new sales staff while he was gone.

"I knew I would be coming home to a very different company and had to prepare for that," Ben recalls. "When you create the monster, you have to live with it, and I knew I had to respect the decisions my team made. It was tough, but ultimately it was the best thing I could've done for my business – and myself."

Do mistakes happen? Of course they do, but the business won't collapse if your employees are prepared; they will learn from those mistakes and gain the experience needed to do a better job the next time. Owners will gain the confidence that comes from learning there's more to running a business than just being in charge. It's also about charting a course and then leading.

Ben puts it very eloquently: "A good leader knows how to delegate, but a good, successful company will delegate for the leader."

So how do you plan to use your next 90 days?

KEY INSIGHTS

When you get stuck in the minutia of working in your business, you will fall into the pit of simply creating a job for yourself – rather than being a business owner. Business owners who take the time to work on their business can structure it in such a way that they could leave it completely in the hands of their employees for 90 days.

- Think about what your business would look like if you left it for 90 days. Does this scenario frighten or excite you?
- Make a list of things that you enjoy doing in your business and a list of things that you don't enjoy doing. Then, make a plan for delegating or outsourcing things you do not enjoy doing.
- Make a list of your strengths and weaknesses as a business owner and then make a plan for filling in the gaps.
- Give your employees leeway to take on more responsibilities, make mistakes, and learn constructively from those mistakes.
- Write down your bucket list – the things you want to do before you "kick the bucket" – in your personal life, and then make a plan to start checking things off.

PRINCIPLE EIGHTEEN

Your Business, Your Passion

By Ed Reid, TAB Facilitator / Coach, York, United Kingdom

Pas-sion [pash-un]
Noun
[1] Any powerful or compelling feeling, such as love or hate.
[2] Strong amorous feeling of love.

Groundhog Day
Noun
[1] In North America on the 2nd of February, when the groundhog is said to come out of its hole at the end of hibernation. If the animal sees its shadow – if the weather is sunny – it goes back into its hole, which portends six more weeks of winter weather.
[2] A situation in which a series of unwelcome or tedious events appear to be recurring in exactly the same way.

O n the face of it, passion and Groundhog Day have nothing in common. We all know both feelings – and they couldn't be more different. But to me, they're two concepts that sum up exactly what running your own business is all about.

I recently came across an article tagged by LinkedIn as a "must-read." Like most people, "must read" for me means 'I would quite like to read it, but don't have the time, so I'll try and come back to it later, but I probably never will.' This one was different though – the title was "'Do What You Love' is Horrible Advice.[1]" Because that title is diametrically opposed to what I believe, I simply had to read it immediately.

The author's premise is that people will rarely pay you for what you're passionate about. He continues by saying that starting a business based on a passion "has probably resulted in more failed businesses than all the recessions combined." What you have to do instead, is to find a business – or a career – that is commercially viable. You work at that business, job, or career and as you build competence, and ultimately expertise, then the passion will eventually come.

The article continues: "Passion is not something that you follow; passion is something that will follow you as you put in the hard work."

To his basic premise, I say, Nonsense! Allow me to explain why.

THE IMPORTANCE OF PASSION IN BUSINESS

One of the things I love most about working with and coaching private business owners is spending my days with people who are absolutely passionate about what they do. They're passionate about their businesses, and delivering on their promises to provide excellent service to their customers.

In *Hunting in a Farmer's World*[2], John Dini tells the story of Chaz Neely, owner of a wholesale supplier of steel products. With the Savings and Loan crisis in the 1980s, Neely's business was hit very hard. He had to go home one night and inform his wife that the only way the business could survive was for them to sell their house and move into an apartment. He pulled the company through the business downturn and returned again to home ownership.

He ran a strong business as a result of fighting his way through the recession and returned the business to one of rapid growth and strong profitability. Neely saw an opportunity to make a big growth leap by adding a new product line and expanding his territory. He was shocked to find that his banker would not give him an additional loan. They felt that he was growing fast enough and expanding further would stretch him too much. Neely went home that night and made an announcement: "Honey, we have to sell the house again!"

Chaz could have easily given up on his dream of being a successful business owner – if it wasn't the passion he felt for growing it. And entrepreneurs (and, at times, their families) have to make these kinds of personal decisions every day. Because when you are passionate about what you do, what you've created, it's not just business – it's personal.

Make no mistake, we all have days in which we feel like Bill Murray's character Phil, in *Groundhog Day*, where we roll out of bed in the morning and think: *Oh no, another damn meeting with so-and-so today.* Even the most passionate owner has that Groundhog Day feeling once in a while. But, when you have passion for your work, it will pull you through those Groundhog Days. And that is what will differentiate you from your competition.[3]

Start a business or a career *without* passion and what happens? You end up echoing the words of Thoreau: "The mass of men lead lives of quiet desperation and go to the grave with the song still in

> *Start a business or a career without passion and what happens? You end up echoing the words of Thoreau: "The mass of men lead lives of quiet desperation and go to the grave with the song still in them."*

them." You end up sitting in a traffic jam on the wrong road thinking to yourself, *there has to be something better than this.*

Well, there is. It's running your own business. And it's your passion that will make your business succeed.

WHAT IF THERE IS NO PASSION FOR YOUR BUSINESS?

I don't find many owners who started their own businesses from scratch who lack passion for it. The passion comes from different places for different owners.

- Some owners absolutely love the role they play in the business. Whether they are "chief evangelizer" or the top engineer in the firm, it's the activities they do on a daily basis that drives their passion.
- Some owners love the product or service they offer. This is common in socially-driven companies, where their business exists for a social purpose. They always have tremendous passion for the social cause.
- Some owners love the people side of their business. They have tremendous loyalty to their teams and create a family-like atmosphere in their business.

- Other owners derive their passion from customers. They never grow tired of hearing from a customer how delighted they were with the product, service or customer service they received.

But, there are some owners who just aren't very passionate about their business. This can sometimes happen with multi-generational businesses. The founders – the parents or grandparents – had the passion. The children are now running the business and lack this same passion. That's a real problem. My advice to them is to find some area in the business they can derive passion from. If they just aren't able to muster up any real passion, then they should think about turning the business over to someone that is passionate about it.

WHAT IF YOUR PASSION IS WANING?

Sometimes owners have lost the bounce in their step they once had. Have you found yourself sitting in your office feeling bored to death? Do you find yourself sleeping in, taking your time coming to the office or being absent more than normal? If you have lost the passion for your business, you can be assured your employees have as well.

Fortunately, there are ways to deal with owner burnout. Here are some of the most common problems and solutions that can keep you from reigniting the fire.[3]

- **You are spending too much time on business minutia or tasks you don't enjoy.** Do you fix your own broken toilet or do you hire a plumber? Hire the team and then delegate. Spend YOUR time improving the business or increasing revenues.

- **Perfectionism.** Not everything has to be done perfectly. No client meeting tomorrow morning? Then your desk does not have to be perfect when you leave tonight. If no one can see the back side of the display, then it doesn't need to look great. Spend your time where it really counts and get some hours back in your day.

- **You are the Chief Problem Solver.** Inevitably problems will arise, but you can minimize them and their impact. Establish documented processes. Having everyone do everything the same way eliminates rework and recovery efforts.

- **Minimize multitasking.** Once thought to be a great business skill, multitasking can result in inefficiency. Focus and finish as much as possible. You will get more things checked off your to-do list, which is good for your business and provides a sense of satisfaction.

- **Realize that YOU need to take care of YOU.** Get adequate sleep, eat less junk food, cut back on caffeine and maybe even throw in some exercise. A bedraggled body is more susceptible to the ravages of burnout.

- **Make time to work ON your business instead of always being buried IN it.** Find the time–30 minutes before leaving home in the morning, a two-hour coffee shop stop once a week or a day away from the office once a month. Pick what will work for you and put it on your calendar. No other appointments and no cancelling it! Work on your business strategy and plans during this time. You will be a more satisfied and productive business owner.

- **Have some FUN!** Celebrate business successes and recognize achievements. You don't have to throw big company-wide parties. A short email celebrating a great sales day adds a smile and some motivation for everyone. Also, give yourself a regularly scheduled "day-off"–no cheating–get totally away from work, no email, no phone calls. The mental separation will really recharge your batteries.

- **Support at home.** Owning a business is a family affair. It takes a special type of relationship and mindset from those who live with you every day. Don't shelter them from it. That can make things worse. Instead, talk to them about your business–solicit and listen to their input. Who knows you better than they do? Get ideas on how they can contribute to the business and solutions to your work/life balance.

KEY INSIGHTS

If you expect your business to succeed you must bring a level of passion to the mission and reason behind why you started a business in the first place. Otherwise, be prepared to find yourself stuck in a Groundhog Day life and attitude. In order to truly run and grow a successful business, you need to have passion.

- Passion is the key for your business to realize its full potential.
- Passion can be derived from many different sources including your daily work activities, your product or service, your employees or your customers.
- If you simply cannot find any passion in your business, perhaps it is time to consider transitioning it to someone who will bring passion to it.
- If you have lost your passion for the business, ways to renew that passion include delegating more, focusing on the strategic areas of the business, creating some fun in the business and seeking support from friends and family.

PRINCIPLE NINETEEN

Run Your Business Like a Franchise

BY MARTIN F. O'NEILL, TAB Facilitator / Coach, Baltimore-Washington Corridor

O ne of the truths about business ownership is businesses that are *less* dependent on their owner being involved in the day-to-day operations are worth more in the marketplace. Yet, most privately-owned businesses are dependent on the owner's involvement and the institutional knowledge of a few key employees.

Investors value businesses that can run smoothly with or without the owner and a few key employees. In my experience working with business owners, the best approach toward increasing the value of your business is to operate it as an Internal Franchise. This provides a great way to improve the performance and value of your business.

In a franchise system a franchisor licenses a business formula—essentially a business operating plan— that provides instruction to the franchisee. The franchisee agrees to operate the business accordingly, while paying the franchisor a percentage of sales as a royalty. Although the franchisee is working within a well-defined framework, he or she also has latitude to act in the best interest of the business as long as it's beneficial to the franchisee and franchisor.

In an Internal Franchise model a company grants authorization of an operational model to entrepreneurial employees who are then trained, mentored, and coached to operate the business at the highest level of proficiency. In a franchise system, the franchise agreement is a binding legal contract. In an Internal Franchise, it's the company's culture that serves as the franchise agreement.

When you turn your business over to your employees and teach them how to operate it using an established model, you are empowering them to run a business that doesn't require your constant attention. Additionally, it frees up your time and increases the value of your business in the eyes of potential investors and buyers—a vital, and effective framework, given today's competitive and rapidly changing business environment.

ESTABLISHING THE INTERNAL FRANCHISE

Having a solid business design is not enough to operate an Internal Franchise. You also need employees who can effectively execute an operational model that is not so dependent on "what you do" but "how you do it" – and why.

The first step to building an Internal Franchise is to

document your operating model in language that existing and new employees can easily follow. This means you need to take time to understand and challenge any fundamental assumptions you have about your business, your industry, and your customers.

Formalizing the operating procedures in this way is also a great way to identify waste, optimize processes and make your business model as streamlined as possible. As Albert Einstein once said, "Everything should be made as simple as possible, but not simpler."

In order to sufficiently document your operating model, you need to make key business decisions along the customer, economic, and operational dimensions of your business. You can then begin to design and implement processes to accomplish your business objectives using your operational model as a guide to implement the following:

- Provide a choreographed outline to your employees to help them understand their individual roles within the larger context of the organization. This helps them work together to achieve your vision for the business.
- Create a reward system as an incentive to help motivate employees.
- Teach employees about the operational structure of your business – how it works and makes money.
- Re-engineer your processes to ensure they produce the results you want.

In short, you can ensure the policies, procedures, processes, and structures of your business work seamlessly together to achieve your business objectives.

VIEWING YOUR EMPLOYEES AS ENTREPRENEURS

Engaged entrepreneurial employees are the second component of an Internal Franchise. When you hire new employees, do you want technicians or entrepreneurs? Rather than hiring people primarily with the specific skills required for the position, I recommend looking for entrepreneurs with an aptitude for the job they will perform, and who will also be on the lookout for ways to do things better.

I believe most people want the opportunity to act like an owner, but are rarely given the chance. As a result, they become conditioned to think like a technician; viewing themselves as a salesperson, engineer, or a manager.

If you want to help your employees avoid this pitfall, start to view them like entrepreneurs. A good place to start is with the hiring process, where you can explain to prospective candidates how they will be given the opportunity to act like an owner—a surprise perk that will awaken the entrepreneur in them. You hired your employees to do a job, so don't try to do it for them.

Michael Benker, a TAB member and owner of Banner Fire Equipment, said many business owners, including himself, spend

> *Rather than hiring people primarily with the specific skills required for the position, I recommend looking for entrepreneurs with an aptitude for the job they will perform who will also be on the lookout for ways to do things better.*

too much time micro-managing. "I feel that I have to have (some) knowledge of every phase of our business, from accounting to service to sales. But, I have learned that I need to let go. This goes back to the idea of hiring good people you can trust to manage things themselves."

Given the opportunity, most employees will act like stewards of their company and, in the most favorable situations, like owners of your business. By shifting the dynamics between you and your employees, you create a culture of ownership and loyalty in which all parties reap some benefits of being entrepreneurs.

For most business owners letting go of responsibility is often the most difficult part of the process. Expectations and account-ability are a big part of making this step successful for you and your employees. "Being explicitly clear about what is expected of employees, and then holding people accountable for those expec-tations is crucially important to the success of your business," advises Bill Vrettos, a long-time TAB Facilitator / Coach.

If you have your operating model in place and hire employees that you believe can eventually take on more responsibility them-selves, you will be well on your way to establishing an Internal Franchise.

INTERNAL FRANCHISE CULTURE

The final step is to nurture the Internal Franchise as the culture of your company. As the owner, you can do this by creating a corporate culture that enforces shared principles and values, and establishes accepted behavior for all members of the organiza-tion. A successful ownership culture compels everyone to think and act like an owner of the business; enforcing the Law of the Entrepreneur:

What's good for the business is good for the entrepreneur,
and what's good for the entrepreneur is good for the business.

An ownership culture is a bond that is cast in trust among the constituent members of the organization. Will new employees, acting as entrepreneurs, make some mistakes? Of course they will. But, they will ultimately become more valuable employees. When you create a strong, empowered culture, it compels people to act with the best interest of the company in mind. It fosters an environment where all the people in the organization feel like they own their franchised operation and act accordingly.

Your employees will be looking to you to be the leader in this ownership culture. As the leader of your organization, it's your responsibility to ensure that your employees engage in and receive continued opportunities for professional development. In return,

What's good for the business is good for the entrepreneur, and what's good for the entrepreneur is good for the business.

they will become a greater asset to your organization and feel a deeper sense of purpose in their professional development and loyalty to the company.

Bono, the lead singer of the Irish rock band U2, sums up the difference between those who develop and nurture entrepreneurial cultures and those who don't this way: "It has been said that after meeting with the great British Prime Minister William

Ewart Gladstone, you are left feeling he was the smartest person in the world, but after meeting with his rival Benjamin Disraeli, you left thinking you were the smartest person.[1]"

KEY INSIGHTS

Business ownership comes with perks and pressures. Establishing a culture of ownership inside your workforce can relieve some of that pressure. Creating an Internal Franchise inside your company will improve the operation of your business, resulting in a culture where employees thrive and improve the value of your business to potential investors.

- Increase the value of your business by developing an Internal Franchise that is not dependent on you and a few key employees.
- Document all processes and protocols into an operating model that is easy for employees to understand and follow.
- Develop an ownership culture with your employees by setting expectations and holding people accountable to those expectations.

PRINCIPLE TWENTY

Business by The Numbers: Managing Your Business using Key Performance Indicators

BY TOM MORTON, TAB Facilitator / Coach, Harrogate, United Kingdom

I f you were a pilot, you would never hop into a plane and fly blindly, without direction or a chart to help you map out your destination and show, in real time, what direction you were steering the plane. Well, the same can be said of charting the course for your business.

While a pilot uses height, speed, and orientation in his operations, a business owner uses Key Performance Indicators (KPIs). KPIs are a performance measurement that provides insight into the critical metrics of a business. When broken down, the term is simply:

- **Key:** The element of gaining a competitive advantage or a make or break component to success or failure.
- **Performance:** Measurable, quantifiable and easily influenced by individual behaviour.
- **Indicator:** Information on past, present, or future performance.

The right KPIs provide a clear understanding for how a business is progressing or is expected to perform in the future. The best KPIs provide a snapshot of success for the business and are rooted in the vision of the organization. They are defined, measurable and tied to key business processes and operational activity that supports the company's overall goals.

Previously in my career when I ran an accounting firm, the financial statements that we produced or audited for our clients were views **into the past.** Airplane controls, which are real-time and constantly changing, show what's happening **in the present.** The good news with KPIs is that you can look not only at the past – and the present – but, if you use the right tools, you **can peer into the future.** Getting a peek into the future empowers you to alter your course and positively affect the future outcome.

KEY KPIs

What's most important when defining KPIs is that you be as specific as possible and create realistic targets. For instance, you may not want to set a KPI of "popular among affluent customers" because measuring affluence can be unreliable. Similarly, you wouldn't want to design a KPI for increasing customer satisfaction unless you had a way to measure and track that component, such as a validated survey system.

There is a range of possibilities to measure a variety of metrics. Here are the main types of KPIs for you to consider:

- **Profitability** measures include sales revenue, gross margin, overhead, and net profit. Measure actual numbers against goals and past results, as well as competitors and industry standards.
- **Efficiency** measures include use of time, use of people, use of physical assets (machines, property) and use of financial assets (inventory turnover, receivables collection, payables credit).
- **Capacity** measures include the amount of warehouse usage or storage tank availability.
- **Opportunity** measures include the number of inquiries, estimates, and orders received by a company. Good opportunity tracking includes your company's conversion rates at each stage of the sales funnel.
- **Liquidity** measures include cash flow forecast, current asset ratio, and your quick ratio.
- **Trend** measures track moving figures over a 12-month period for KPIs such as sales, margin and orders.

KPIs for Your Business

There are no "standard" KPIs that apply to all companies. Sales, profits and cash are numbers every business tracks, but they only tell you the results of your efforts – and these metrics provide a look into the past. If you're asking yourself what KPIs should my business use, the answer, of course, depends on what it is that you're trying to evaluate. I can tell you, from experience, that there are some basic ground rules that always apply:

1. Don't use too many KPIs. Too many lessens the focus on the really important KPIs. **Keep it simple**. Get good at

tracking a few, then (if you need to) add more. If you find that a tracked KPI is adding no value, get rid of it.

2. Create KPIs that are **easy to calculate** so everyone on your team can use them to make timely decisions.

3. Strive to track KPIs that relate to **events happening in the present...**

4. ...while also tracking current **indicators that will influence future outcomes**. These are known as **leading indicators**. For example, lead flow is a leading indicator to future sales.

5. Don't overlook the **importance of non-financial indicators**, such as the number of inquiries from your website or number of customer service tickets.

6. **A picture tells a thousand words** – especially when it comes to trends. Your 12-month moving totals for sales and margin, if shown in graphical form, will pick up a trend far earlier than the figures themselves.

7. Consider using a **dashboard**—a display optimization tool—to keep your company KPIs organized in one place where it is easy to view and analyze the information.

Take your time deciding what your KPIs should be. Once you start using KPIs, it's important to regularly communicate them to your employees. While some owners are initially apprehensive, my experience is that this helps most employees better align their own work activities with the goals and performance of the company. You should also incorporate KPIs into your performance management system, which may be tied to incentives, raises or profit distributions.

KEY INSIGHTS

Key Performance Indicators are very effective business management tools. Without them, you really have no clear picture of how your business is performing or where your performance is headed. Take the time to determine what KPIs are important for your business success and implement a process to measure and update them regularly. This will be invaluable to the overall success of your business, because it is true that we manage what we measure!

- Using KPIs to measure your company's performance can help you determine the areas in which your company is performing well and those that need attention.
- Take time to determine which KPIs will be most helpful to your business performance. Start with a few KPIs and then add to them.
- Include leading, lagging, and trend indicators in your KPI dashboard.
- Update your employees on performance of your KPIs so they can better align their work activities with the priorities and performance of the overall business.

PRINCIPLE TWENTY-ONE

Your Hidden Strategic Advantage: Technology as Your Core Competency

By **Kalar Rajendiran**, TAB Facilitator / Coach, San Mateo County, California

As we reflect on the 25-year history of TAB, we asked facilitators and members who have been part of TAB for over two-decades, what they believe is the most significant change business has seen since 1990. As you might imagine, the resounding universal answer was technology. Here are a few of their thoughts on how business was run, and done, in the late 20th century.

"It used to take so long to do things that aren't even part of a job description now. International communications were a disaster. Does anyone remember Telex? We used

135

Telex to send orders to the UK. It was a little machine that punched holes into inch-wide paper. The holes were then transferred as beeps on the phone. Then came the fax machine. One of the most fantastic inventions at the time!" John F. Dini, TAB Facilitator / Coach and author

"Everything was printed and mailed. Color photography for marketing and advertising was very expensive. We'd have to spend lots of money on photo shoots, transparencies, design, etc. How it's done now is a total switch from how it used to be done." Lynn Gastineau, owner of Gastineau Log Homes

Probably the most important change in technology in the past 25 years is that technology is now often a competitive advantage in many different industries, including some you wouldn't expect.

A MEMBER STORY

I want to share a story about a TAB member company that transformed itself within an industry that the general public does not associate with high tech. The story is of particular significance, as it is a mature industry. For purposes of this story I'll refer to the TAB member as Michael. Michael runs a specialty construction services business.

In the thick of the most recent recession, Michael shared in a board meeting that he did not know what he was going to do to take his business to the next level. **But, he is committed to build a competitive edge, transform his company and become a leader in his market.**

The ensuing board discussion, based on Michael's challenge, revealed the business demanded Michael's constant attention.

Even basic tasks such as ordering the right materials at the right time and delivering them to the correct job site required the owner's involvement. The successful completion of a project also depended on ensuring clear, consistent and timely communication between the drywall assembly/finishing crew, lath/plaster crew, carpentry services crew and door and hardware crew working on the project. Any mix-ups caused cost-overruns and delays, potentially jeopardizing the project itself.

USING TECHNOLOGY TO CREATE ADVANTAGE

Based on the advice of his peer board, Michael launched a strategic initiative to capture the entire operational process inside of a software application to improve the consistency and efficiency of his operations, making it less dependent on his direct involvement.

- Management by Exception (MBE) is a principle whereby a manager is notified only when actual results significantly deviate from set expected results. MBE was adopted as the strategic management principle that he used to run the business.
- A management software tool was identified as the best way to implement MBE and provide Michael with the tools to set the expected norms, run a more predictable business and have complete control and visibility over all of his projects.

If actual performance on a job deviates significantly from the norm, the software notifies Michael that an "exception has occurred." He then gets involved to rapidly resolve the issue and get the project back on track. An additional benefit of the software is that it empowers employees with more authority, increasing their motivation level. With the solution in place, Michael is now free to focus his time and energy on the strategic aspects of the business. He only needs to get involved when exceptions occur.

Because Michael was willing to trust a new technological solution, it freed him up to move the business forward. As a result:

1. The business, initially, achieved a net margin a few percentage points above the industry norm; and the margins continue to increase as the company enhances the software application and on-boards more of its employees.
2. Revenue grew significantly since the company no longer has any operational or quality control issues that previously hurt its profitability.
3. This implementation provides a potential opportunity to license this software application to other businesses within the construction industry.

FINDING YOUR TECHNOLOGICAL COMPETITIVE ADVANTAGE

Some readers may find Michael's story interesting, but do not see how it applies to them, especially if they are not in the technology field. Given the importance of technology to almost all industries these days, there may be an opportunity to identify a technological advantage in your business. To start thinking about this, here are some questions to ask yourself:

- **Big Data:** Have you collected, analyzed and made decisions based on all the various data that you have across all areas of your business? Have you developed an approach to data collection and analysis that allows you to continue to innovate your business based on new insights?

- **Communication and Collaboration:** Have you integrated social media and collaboration technology into your business? Do your employees communicate better as a result? Do you collaborate with your customers using this technology?
- **Workforce Management:** Like Michael, have you developed processes, know-how or leveraged technology to manage projects and people?
- **Marketing:** Do you successfully incorporate digital channels, such as search engines, display networks, online advertising, social media and mobile platforms, into growing your brand, managing your reputation and generating leads?
- **Multi-Media:** Have you successfully incorporated multimedia, such as testimonial videos and video blogs, to provide transparency into your business?
- **Business App:** Have you developed a successful app for your business that your customers use on a regular basis? Can this app be generalized to open up new product lines or channels for your business?

KEY INSIGHTS

In today's tech-driven world, we have tools available to us like never before. We can either elect to adopt technology and use it to create a competitive advantage, or we can ignore it and be left behind. If technology is not a competitive advantage for your business, it probably can be. If Michael was able to achieve this in the construction business, chances are you can as well.

- Technology has developed dramatically over the last 25 years, forever changing the way we do business in every industry.
- There are many ways you can integrate technology into running your business, from operations and workforce management to marketing communications.
- While appropriately-applied technology can be a strategic advantage in your own business, your innovation may also create an opportunity to sell your solution to other non-competitive industries, creating a completely new revenue stream.
- Especially if you are not tech-savvy, a great way to uncover your own technological competitive advantage is to participate in a group of business advisors from diverse backgrounds and industries.

PRINCIPLE TWENTY-TWO

Why Emotional Decision Making is Killing Your Business and How to Stop It

By **CAROL CRAWFORD,** TAB Facilitator / Coach, Grand Rapids, Michigan

T he trickiest thing about emotional decision-making is that it is very difficult to recognize. When your business is your baby, you are inevitably going to be emotionally tied to it. The real problem comes when you ignore this fact and plunge onward without taking a step back and looking at the decision from an outsider's perspective. This is incredibly hard to do, but crucial to the long-term success of your business.

As a business grows, an owner will need to add new staff. An inexperienced owner may look to family and friends for help based on existing relationships in which a level of trust already exists. The owner may believe that by hiring friends and family he or she is developing a strong "family" bond with their employees, leading the owner to feel secure about the team.

A MEMBER STORY

Everything may be fine, initially, but often trouble is just around the corner. For example, Mary, a TAB member who started her business with the financial assistance of family members. As the business grew she added family and friends to her staff. But rather than treating them like employees, she treated them like she would her family and friends.

If someone was a little late to work, left a little early, or talked on their mobile phone a lot she said nothing. In her mind she rationalized that same employee would stay a little late or take work home during a pinch when asked and without reporting the additional time they worked. But over time, Mary realized the number of "lost" hours in a workday among her employees was excessive and climbing.

Additionally, the employee handbook stated company equipment, such as computers or mobile phones, were not to be used for personal use. Yet, there were no consequences when someone did. Employees routinely took selfies in the office, texted excessively and shopped online during the workday.

Over time, Mary found her employees, many of whom were financial backers, were stuck in "yesterday's thinking" where they believed their informal behavior was acceptable. Mary wanted to move the business forward, yet she found the employee culture, which she allowed to be established, was a roadblock to progress and growth. But she also wondered how she could challenge those who had been supportive in helping her start her business. Such issues led Mary to rethink whether taking out a bank loan for financing was preferred over relying on friends and family to fund the business – and the baggage that came along with this obligation.

Mary made some initial attempts to gain more control, much as a parent would when asking a child to stop misbehaving before the parent counted to ten. In employee meetings she casually mentioned the need to be more productive, which resulted in no change in her employees behavior. Fearful her employees might get mad, quit or not like her any more she considered offering a bonus program for increased productivity and accuracy rather than tackling the problem head on.

> *Such issues led Mary to rethink whether taking out a bank loan for financing was preferred over relying on friends and family to fund the business – and the baggage that came along with this obligation.*

Making an Objective Decision

Mary finally decided that the "family" atmosphere had gone too far. Her customers were not receiving prompt service, there was an increase in quoting and billing errors, and the additional staff were not generating the additional revenue she thought they would. She decided to bring her challenge to her board.

Mary's TAB board convinced her to take control of her company and its employees and remove her emotions from the situation. They reminded her that she was running a business, not a family and friends get-together. If she expected her business to survive and thrive, she would need to take control of the organization and run it professionally.

Emboldened by the support of other business owners who had been through similar challenges in their own companies, Mary followed up with her employees as a group, and individually, to review her company's updated work rules. The transition wasn't easy at first and Mary had trouble addressing infractions as they occurred. However, her board supported her each month as she built her skills and confidence in running her company in a more efficient and effective manner.

As a result of these changes, Mary's company has enjoyed a 67 percent increase in growth, profitability has increased, and she feels confident in her staff's abilities to run the company when she takes time off for herself.

This story is focused on employee issues, which is one of the most common emotional issues we see from business owners at TAB. However, it's easy to slip into making emotional decisions about every facet of your business. Financing, growth, exit or succession planning all have the potential for being highly emotional for the business owner.

TAB member and owner of Banner Fire Equipment Michael Benker advises, "Ensure you are educated and prepared. Business decisions need to be based on facts, not emotions. So make sure you have the data and you know how to analyze it, so you can make the decision."

THE UNIQUE EMOTIONAL CHALLENGES OF FAMILY BUSINESSES

The key issues of family businesses are similar to those of any closely tied organization. However, emotional decision making has the potential to seep into a family-owned business environment because they are wholly integrated within the family. Family businesses encompass traditional business objectives as well as intricate affairs of family relationships. Family businesses are constantly forced to confront the difference between decisions that are made in the best interest of the family versus the best interest of the business.

When family members work together emotions can interfere with business decisions and issues may arise as relatives see the business from different perspectives. Those engaged in daily operations are more likely to be concerned about production and output, while family members who are "silent" partners are focused on the bottom line. Other challenges are also likely to arise when non-family employees enter the picture. Owners must be prepared to deal with competition among family members surrounding issues such as adequate compensation and job titles.

Family businesses that place "family first" often adopt a decision making process primarily based on emotion. Change is difficult within this philosophy as decisions are ultimately made to ensure relationship stability and conflict avoidance. In contrast, family businesses that operate using a "business first" mentality tend to be focused on the service and/or product aspects of the operation. As a result, these businesses tend to place a great deal of emphasis on productivity and competitiveness and decisions are usually made based on exploiting new opportunities and embracing the change that typically accompanies growth and survival.

Which management philosophy yields the best results? Both have their pros and cons and there are no surefire management principles or techniques that will guarantee success. The key is to anticipate conflict knowing it will occur at some point and then use it as a learning opportunity to clearly communicate your philosophy to family and non-family employees. If the fundamental differences between emotions and objectives are properly balanced, the potential for conflict is reduced and can result in a positive culture for family and employees alike.

Key Insights

As a business owner, it's easy to become emotionally involved in making key decisions. But making these decisions based on your feelings, or those of others, can lead to bad results. It's important you take the time to pause and make sure you're making a decision based on facts. Relying on gut instincts will serve you in some areas of life, but not when it comes to making important business decisions. As Edward Deming advises "in God we trust, all others bring data."

- As business owners we are all, on some level, emotionally tied to our businesses. This exposes us to the possible pitfalls of emotional decision-making.
- Start by recognizing when a decision is emotionally charged and take the time to step back and try to look at it from an outsider's perspective.
- Educate yourself and be prepared with the analysis and facts needed to make a sound business decision.
- When conflict does occur and emotions are high in a business decision, use the situation as a learning opportunity with family and staff to improve culture and reduce emotions in future decisions.

PRINCIPLE TWENTY-THREE

Achieving Predictable Income Using a Subscription Model in Any Industry

BY JACQUELYN GERNAEY, TAB Facilitator / Coach, Suffolk County, New York

I f you're anything like me, you enjoy the convenience of having movies delivered to your home via the Netflix subscription service, which founders Reed Hastings and Marc Randolph developed in the late 1990s. The two put a clever spin on the model of subscription-based product purchasing that emerged during the 18th century when publishers of newspapers, magazines, and books began offering access to content delivered to a customer's home on a recurring basis. The key to success of the subscription-based model is subscribers make a commitment to use your service or product for a specific length of time.

Few readers may remember an era in which ice, milk and other dairy products were delivered to consumers' homes before individual refrigeration systems became commonplace. These early subscription services, however, were invaluable models allowing businesses to scale based on committed revenue while also being cost effective to customers.

Rather than selling products individually, some companies choose to sell their products or access to a service on a recurring basis—usually monthly. While the subscription model is not new, what is new in the subscription economy is the diversity of businesses that are either launching with a subscription model or converting an existing business to this model.

Software packages, for example, used to require a large upfront capital cost with a small monthly fee for maintenance. Salesforce.com changed the entire industry by providing a web-hosted Customer Relationship Management (CRM) platform, with no upfront investment. Instead, customers commit to a year of service and pay a monthly fee for use. This model presents a lower barrier to entry for new customers and is more lucrative for the subscription provider.

If you're thinking, "this will not work with my product or service," try to maintain an open mind. Subscription models *are* working for all kinds of different types of businesses. It may take some creativity as well as trial and error to figure out how you're able to adapt your service or product to the new subscription economy.

HOW CAN YOU EXCEL IN THE NEW SUBSCRIPTION ECONOMY?

In his book *The Automatic Customer*[1], John Warrillow advises entrepreneurs that anyone from a home contractor to a local florist can build a subscription service into their business using various creative models including:

- **Adding a Discovery Element:** Most people are not used to discovering new products through a subscription model. NatureBox is starting to change this by selling healthy snacks for kids delivered to their customers' doors monthly. As part of their marketing campaign, they promise to introduce customers to a new snack each month.

- **Considering a Social Purpose:** Savvy subscription businesses appeal to convenience, but don't stop there. They also appeal to their customers' desire for a company to give back to the communities they serve by donating meals, clothing, school supplies or other services to local, national or global nonprofit organizations.

- **Emphasizing Convenience.** Any consumable product is ripe for a subscription model. Families with babies, for example, welcome having diapers show up at their door. There is nothing worse than running out of this necessity.

- **Emphasizing Variety.** There are a number of subscription models that emphasize the element of surprise. Subscribers do not know what they are going to actually receive. The monthly Birchbox package of beauty products is tailored to their subscribers' preferences, and also include a variety of product types and brands.

- **Emphasizing Simplicity.** This is a key element for any business, but especially critical for a subscription service. A sure way to receive cancellations is for your subscription service to require effort by your customers. If your product or service does involve an element of complexity, be sure to include a "how it works" page on your website.

SUBSCRIPTION MODEL EXAMPLES

Retail: One of the best examples of a subscription model is Amazon.com's add-on service Amazon Prime. When the Prime subscription service was added, the value proposition for customers seemed a bit perplexing because the Amazon store is open to everyone. The hook with the Amazon Prime service, however, is customers receive their purchases in two days—and in our instant gratification culture this is huge.

Some analysts estimate Amazon.com has as many as 50 million customers worldwide. When the international retailer raised its Prime subscription price from $79 per year to $99, there was little pushback from subscribers.

The addition of Prime sounded like a great new offering to Amazon customers, but the company clearly knew what it was doing. Prime turned out to be the Trojan Horse, moving Amazon deeper into the homes and wallets of its customers. Experts report the average Prime member now spends double the amount a non-member spends on purchases each year.

Professional Services: Nothing terrifies a professional services business owner more than having employees sitting on the bench collecting a paycheck while waiting for the next client. When business is plentiful, everyone is happy. Employees are productive and the owner is generating positive cash flow. When things slow down, however, there is a lot of cash going out, but little coming in. The business cannot survive in this mode for very long. The way to stave off the highs and lows in professional services is by converting to a subscription model.

Professional services organizations have a lot of knowledge capital and can potentially use their expertise creatively to add or convert to a subscription model. The professional services subscription model was started by businesses who did market and/ or competitive research in specific industries. Their clients valued their information and would subscribe to it. Other models are possible. For example, a manufacturing business having trouble hiring and retaining qualified talent might be willing to pay a monthly fee for recruiters to locate technical school graduates in their area.

USING A HYBRID APPROACH

Using a traditional pricing approach with a subscription model is a good way to make the transition. If, for example, you install alarm systems, build elevators or sell windows, think about how you can add a subscription element to the existing service you're providing, such as alarm monitoring, annual inspections or offering a quarterly window cleaning service. If you're able to tie two services together and make a higher profit on the subscription end of the business, it will allow you to reduce your prices on the transactional portion of your business.

Eric Aschinger, a TAB member and owner of Aschinger Electric, uses this model in his business. "We have a lot of day-to-day contracts and this will likely never change. But, there is a lot of opportunity for renewable jobs," he says, adding, "We're looking to move more and more customers to a subscription model using maintenance contracts. Some will be monthly and others will be annual, depending on the product and service package."

KEY INSIGHTS

In today's go, go, go environment, people are busy and many don't have the time, or desire, to keep up with monthly tasks such as remembering to buy dog food or pay the bill for a home security system. This is an opportunity for your business. You can help simplify the lives of your customers by providing these types of services on a recurring basis. They fill a void and allow you to up-sell or cross-sell other products while maintaining a predicable income stream. Remember, to stay in business with the new changing economy, you need to be creative in your business approach. The owners of Blockbuster Video certainly wish they had given more thought to Netflix when Netflix entered the movie rental business.

- A subscription model will level out the high and low trends most business owners experience by developing a model to generate consistent monthly revenue.
- Using a little creativity, most any business in any industry can convert to the subscription model of business.
- Consider building a specialty model around Discovery, Variety, Convenience or Simplicity.
- Focus on the customer first and foremost, employing a great on-boarding process and emphasizing the specific differentiator that your service provides.
- Best of all, use the subscription model to make lots of money!

PRINCIPLE TWENTY-FOUR

The Strategic Advantage of Market Intelligence

BY BOB DODGE, TAB Facilitator / Coach,
Denver, Colorado

I f you ask a typical business owner to define "marketing", it will include developing marketing collateral, a website and perhaps social media programs. What the typical marketing definition will rarely include is market intelligence and segmentation. Businesses with a strong handle on market demographics, geography, competitive analysis, preferred distribution channels, and buying patterns, have a distinct advantage over businesses that don't intimately know their market.

SOCCER MOMS

According to Wikipedia, the phrase soccer mom generally refers to a married middle-class North American woman who lives in the suburbs and has school age children. She is sometimes portrayed in the media as busy or overburdened and driving a minivan or SUV. She is also portrayed as putting the interests of her family, and most importantly her children, ahead of her own. The phrase derives from the literal, specific description of a mother who transports and watches her children play soccer. This term came into widespread use during the 1996 US presidential election.

When someone hears the term "soccer mom", it provides all kinds of associations. The various profile characteristics of the term don't need to be described because the term does that itself. This is efficient. It is valuable. In the presidential elections, candidates built entire campaigns around appealing to soccer moms. They developed specific messages targeted to them.

The great interest in soccer moms was due to the belief that they were the most important swing vote in the 1996 election. They probably were. Suburban women favored Bill Clinton by a wide margin over Bob Dole.

Clinton's campaign staff knew the market. They ran focus groups and polls and segmented the voter base into groups, including soccer moms. They developed a very thoughtful profile of this segment. By knowing them so well, they were able to develop customized messaging and communicate in the channels they used. Clinton won the election comfortably.[1]

WHY KNOWING YOUR MARKET IS CRITICAL

If you don't know your market, it doesn't matter how you sell them. They won't buy.

Imagine...

- Trying to convince someone to buy a flight to Chicago when they said they wanted to see "Chicago" (the movie).
- Teaching someone to manage people, when they are perfectly content being an engineer, sales rep, manufacturing worker or nurse.
- Selling a six pack of Coca Cola to someone who has expressed a desire to **taste** the New Coke, by showing it to them so they can **look** at it and describing it so they can **hear** about it.

I recall one TAB member wanted to market to his prospects though social media. He felt he was missing an opportunity since there was so much buzz about marketing through this channel. His board asked him to define his customers by industry and demographics. They asked him to describe the companies and the people who actually buy from him now, and how they find him. As he did so, the board helped him realize that few of these people would likely find his company via Twitter because most of them don't use the internet. They barely use computers!

Another TAB member wondered why an employee would not obtain a professional certification, and earn the promised promotion and salary increase. When the employee explained why he had worked hard to lose weight, the member learned what motivated him was to be there for the long-run for his family. His dad had died too young because he was overweight. Being there for his family was his source of motivation, not money or a title. The member realized he did not know his other market: his employees. His TAB board educated him on the importance of understanding the motivations of his employees and how to uncover them.

WHAT TO KNOW ABOUT YOUR MARKET

We miss the boat if we can't answer the following about our markets:

- Who are the companies and the people we are trying to reach (size, location, position, motives, etc.)?
- Where would these prospects go to find us (trade shows, their network, business directory, the internet, etc.)?
- Who is our competition (our prospects' alternatives, even if it means the status quo) and what strengths and weaknesses do they have relative to us?
- What would our prospects want to **hear, see** or **get a feel for** from us in order to move through the buying process (specifications, features, advantages and benefits, stories, etc.)?
- Why would they buy? What would they achieve by buying (fear, risk, pride, fulfillment of a vision, personal dream, etc.)?

The *Why* is critical to understanding your market. If you understand this then you can present your offering in a way that appeals to the needs and interests of your target audience. This allows you to minimize the need for the competitive advantages of features, delivery and pricing. Provided you help them to conceptualize

> *Provided you help them to conceptualize that your product or service satisfies their need, your client will now associate you with solving their problem, achieving their success, and eliminating their pain.*

that your product or service satisfies their need, your client will now associate you with solving their problem, achieving their success, and eliminating their pain.

How would you find out what that need is? Ask, and then listen carefully to what they tell you. Ask more questions to really understand your market. Everyone else will be trying to sell cheap plane tickets and you will be providing a high margin *night on the town* including a great movie!

Key Insights

Knowing your market and positioning your offering to appeal to your market is the pathway to real revenue growth in your business. If you don't know the people you are trying to sell to – their habits, wants, needs, pain points, and buying behavior – chances are you're missing your target market in a very big way. You may think your product or service is great, but if it's not addressing your target market's Why, then there is very little chance of success.

- Get to know your market by defining the demographics, geography, wants, needs, pain points, and buying patterns, as well as developing a thorough competitive analysis.
- Understand what your target market really needs – and especially the Why for making a purchasing decision in your space.
- Speak to your market directly by developing a message specifically for your defined target market that appeals to them and connects with their Why.

PRINCIPLE TWENTY-FIVE

Growth Strategies Don't Just Happen by Accident

By Diana Gats, TAB Facilitator / Coach,
Dallas/Fort Worth, Texas

I f your growth strategy is simply to be cheap, remember, there is always someone else out there willing to go broke faster than you. A sound business will grow based on offering a valuable product or service, not a cheap one.

Growth requires:

- The development of a **Strategy**
- The **Discipline** to plan based on knowledge of the products or services, customer needs, business prospects, and competitors
- The **Metrics** to assess achievement and success

A sound business will grow based on offering a valuable product or service, not a cheap one. Which means you must put as much strategic effort and thought into the expansion of your business as you do into marketing, sales, or operations areas that make up its foundation. Regardless of the stage of your business, growing your business requires a strategy that involves **product evaluation, customer segmentation, people and process evaluation** and establishing the **metrics** to track your growth. Growth in business doesn't just happen on its own.

THE BUSINESS GROWTH CURVE

Businesses typically face different growth-related challenges based on how new or established they are.

New Businesses are focused on getting new customers and clients and bringing in revenue. Often, expenses outweigh sales and it takes a year or two for profits to be generated. In this phase, it is imperative that a sales process be developed and refined for maximum consistency and effectiveness.

At the three to five year mark in a new business sales are likely on track and, as an entrepreneur, you should focus on maximizing profits. It is important to review your business processes to confirm that they can support continued growth. This is an important time to evaluate staffing to be certain that your company is staffed with the right people to continue your growth.

Business owners entering their fifth year or beyond often become complacent if they see their sales plateau or employees become stagnant. Businesses at this stage are susceptible to becoming less innovative and less adaptable to change. They should evaluate all growth-related areas described below and make the necessary changes to return to growth.

PRODUCT EVALUATION AND STRATEGY

The first step in creating a growth strategy is to evaluate your products and services. Ask yourself the following questions:

- Do you have one product or multiple product offerings? Many businesses find that their one product is really 8-10 product and/or service variations that can be expensive to maintain.
- Which of your products provided the highest sales volume? The lowest?
- Which generate the highest profits? The least, or in fact are money losers? You may identify products, services or variations that should be discontinued.
- Do you have constraints within some of your product processes that limit your sales potential?
- Where in your organization do you have extra capacity that can be productively applied?
- Are there areas of the business where outsourcing makes sense? Or conversely, is it time to bring a function or process in house that was performed externally?
- Perhaps it is time to raise prices and/or cut costs? Owners are often reluctant to raise prices and while you should approach this carefully, if you are offering a strong product or service, you are entitled to a fair profit as a result.
- What new products can you offer? Can you offer a subscription service, to generate predictable add-on income, that can complement your core products or services?

It is important that you ask these questions regularly and answer them objectively. Making adjustments to your product mix along the way, and especially at the key points of your business lifecycle, is important to developing a business that continues to grow in size and profitability.

CUSTOMER SEGMENTATION

The next part of developing an intentional growth strategy is evaluating and segmenting your customers. Use the following questions and best practices to segment and evaluate your customers and prospects:

- Segment your customers into well-defined groups based on how they consume your product. The most common segments are business vs. consumer, size, geography, industry and demographics. You could also segment them using other criteria, such as whether they buy directly or through distributors, whether purchasing is centralized or decentralized, etc.

- Once you segment them, assess their needs and usage patterns. How profitable is each segment, How profitable is each segment? How satisfied are they with your product or service? What additional needs do they have that you might be able to fill? This information not only feeds back into your product line evaluation but it also shapes how you market and position yourself with new prospects in those segments.

- What new customers and markets could current products be sold too? Perhaps you specialize in one industry, but there may be other industries where your product would serve a need. Similarly, you may be focused geographically but have an opportunity to expand.

- Who do your customers buy from or could buy from (beyond you) and why? Develop detailed knowledge of your competitors (see "Know, Respect and Leverage Your Competition"). Surveying, focus groups and mystery shopping are effective ways to better understand your customers, prospects and competitors.

- As part of this process, consider other distribution channels for your product or service. Your current or new potential distributors may have access to desirable customer segments that you've not yet tapped.

Going through this process is likely to reveal significant untapped customer segments and product opportunities to significantly contribute to the growth of your business.

PEOPLE AND PROCESSES

As you plan your future growth, the next areas to evaluate are your people and your processes. Ask yourself:

- Do you have the right people in the right positions (see "Right People, Right Seats")?
- Is your sales force good at hunting vs. farming? Make sure to match hunters with hunting roles (acquiring new customers) and farmers with farmer roles (growing existing accounts).
- Do you have sales processes that have the capability to grow your business? You may not have needed much process to get off the ground and established, but achieving predictable and growing revenue will require a mature sales process.
- Do you have a management team that is capable and that work well together? Are you comfortable delegating important decisions to each of your managers in their respective areas?
- Has your business started to form into silos? Do the Sales

and Operations team work well with each other or are they at odds? These types of cultural issues need to be addressed before they become the entrenched culture.

- Are the processes documented and robust enough for training of new personnel and continuing to generate high quality of products?

Your current people and processes may have been sufficient to get your business off the ground and established. But, business owners often find that the people and processes that got them started are not always the same people that can take them to the next stage of growth. Change in people and process is a necessary part to developing a sustainable growth strategy.

METRICS

The last key component to predictable and sustained growth is metrics. If something is not measured, it cannot be improved. See "Business by the Numbers" for best practices on Key Performance Indicators (KPIs). To be successful, your growth decisions must be based on actual facts and data not on emotions or what we believe to be facts.

Metrics are measures put in place to assess actual performance against goals. When actual results to goal are captured, there will be a positive or negative variance. When there is a variance, getting to the root cause reveals whether the variance is related to products, customers, people or process. Understanding the root cause allows for corrective actions to be developed and implemented.

MEMBER EXAMPLE

In 2009, a manufacturer TAB member had revenues of $3

million, and had plateaued at that level for several years. To make matters more concerning, 70% of revenues came from just one customer.

By creating their customer-product matrix, using the questions listed above, they were able to understand their market at a more meaningful level. Using this information, we were able to structure their business in such a way that they were able to sustainably grow by offering new products to the market and attracting new customers. As a result, growth has come from:

- Selling more current products to existing customers
- Selling new products to existing customers
- Selling current products to new customers
- Selling new products to new customers

This member's business has grown to $4.6 million in revenues, and the account that represented 70% of revenues is now at 40%.

KEY INSIGHTS

I have found that business owners who are the most successful are the ones who have discipline in running their business. The discipline to sustain growth includes evaluating and making changes to product and service offerings, customer segments, business process and staff. Disciplined owners evaluate these areas and make changes based on well-defined metrics/KPIs. These decisions can be difficult to make. But those owners that have achieved predictable income and sustainable growth, and continue to take their businesses to the next growth stage, have employed the discipline to develop and follow a strategy to achieve long-term growth.

- There is no shortage of businesses that are able to compete on price. Instead, focus on providing real value to your customers using quality and differentiation tactics.
- Evaluate your people and processes. The people and processes who got you to the current stage of your business may not be the right ones to take you to the next level.
- Use key metrics to understand your product or service and your customers. This knowledge will help you adjust your product offerings and customer segmentation to position your offerings for long-term growth.

THE NEXT 25 YEARS

TAB's core culture is the understanding and promoting of the fact that business decision makers need to bring their team along on the journey with them in order to achieve outstanding business results. I'm very proud of the TAB corporate team, with its great experience and dedication to our TAB culture. The team is aligned with the mission of being agents of change for our members around the world.

It has been an honor to be associated with TAB's certified facilitator / coaches around the world. Their passion for helping business owners is unparalleled.

It is equally rewarding to know we have people who started with us within the first couple of years of TAB's humble beginnings and are still with us today. There is no greater endorsement for a company than member loyalty and longevity. To date, tens of thousands of business owners around the world have used the TAB system to improve their leadership skills and the results in their companies.

My vision for the next 25 years is for TAB to continue to build on our success to date and help an even greater number of businesses around the world. I want TAB to be viewed as the premier organization providing peer-advisory boards and coaching services globally. It would be wonderful if we are all able to celebrate TAB helping business leaders in 50 countries or more by our 50th anniversary.

Here's to the next 25 years of success!

Allen E. Fishman

REFERENCES

PRINCIPLE 3: 90 DAY ONBOARDING

1. Baeklund, Peter. www.peterbaeklund.com
2. Warrillow, John. *The Automatic Customer: Creating a Subscription Business in Any Industry*. Portfolio, 2015.
3. *Tombstone*. Dir. George P. Cosmatos. By Kevin Jarre. Perf. Kurt Russell, Val Kilmer, and Sam Elliott. Hollywood Pictures, 1993.

PRINCIPLE 4: RIGHT PEOPLE RIGHT SEATS

1. Collins, J. *Good to Great: Why Some Companies Make the Leap... And Others Don't*. HarperBusiness, 2001.

PRINCIPLE 5: WRONG ROOM

1. Pentland, A. "Sandy" (2013). *Beyond the Echo Chamber*. Harvard Business Review. www.hbr.org/2013/11/beyond-the-echo-chamber.
2. Bainbridge, Stephen M., Why a Board? Group

Decisionmaking in Corporate Governance. Vanderbilt Law Review, Vol. 55, pp. 1-55, 2002. Available at SSRN: http://ssrn.com/abstract=266683

PRINCIPLE 9: EXIT PLANNING

1. Fishman, Allen. *Strategic Business Leadership: The Proven Formula for Greater Company Success!* Direct communication Services, Inc., 2013.
2. Burlingham, Bo. *Finish Big: How Great Entrepreneurs Exit Their Companies on Top.* Portfolio, 2013.

PRINCIPLE 10: START WITH WHY

1. www.netpromoter.com
2. The Golden Circle, ©2013 Simon Sinek Inc.
3. Bosworth, Michael and Ben Zoldan. *What Great Sales People Do.* McGraw Hill Publishers, 2012.
4. Hernandez, M. Shannon. *Emotional Triggers and Words that Sell.* The Huffington Post 02/10/2015.

PRINCIPLE 11: KNOW YOUR COMPETITION

1. Rumelt, Richard. *Good Strategy Bad Strategy: The Difference and Why It Matters.* Crown Business, 2011.

PRINCIPLE 12: CONFIDENCE

2. Dini, John. *Hunting in a Farmer's World: Celebrating the Mind of an Entrepreneur.* Gardendale Press, 2013.

PRINCIPLE 14: FLEXIBILITY

1. Das, Lama Surya. *Make Me One with Everything: Buddhist Meditations to Awaken from the Illusion of Separation.* Sounds True, 2015.

2. Ries, Eric. *The Lean Startup: How Today's Entrepreneurs Use Continuous Innovation to Create Radically Successful Businesses.* Crown Business, 2011.

PRINCIPLE 16: WORK/LIFE BALANCE

1. Fishman, Allen. *The Alignment Factor: Unlock Potential, Boost Employee Performance, and Increase Profits.* TAB Boards Media, 2013.

PRINCIPLE 18: PASSION

1. Haden, Jeff. *"Do What You Love" Is Horrible Advice.* LinkedIn Posts. www.linkedin.com/pulse/20140602121626-20017018—do-what-you-love-is-horrible-advice.

2. Dini, John. *Hunting in a Farmer's World: Celebrating the Mind of an Entrepreneur.* Gardendale Press, 2013.

3. *Groundhog Day.* Dir. Harold Ramis. Prod. Harold Ramis. By Harold Ramis and Danny Rubin. Perf. Harold Ramis, Bill Murray, and Andie MacDowell. Columbia Pictures, 1993.

4. Cook, Jean. *Business Viewpoint: Avoid business owner burnout with 4 tips.* Tulsa World. 8/21/2014. http://www.tulsaworld.com/business/businessviewpoint/business-viewpoint-avoid-business-owner-burnout-with-tips/article_cc1ee62e-afa6-558e-bf2c-8e63e01f5b1e.html.

PRINCIPLE 19: INTERNAL FRANCHISE

1. Wiseman, Liz. *Multipliers: How the Best Leaders Make Everyone Smarter*. HarperBusiness, 2010.

PRINCIPLE 23: SUBSCRIPTION MODEL

1. Warrillow, John. *The Automatic Customer: Creating a Subscription Business in Any Industry*. Portfolio, 2015.

PRINCIPLE 24: KNOW YOUR MARKET

1. en.wikipedia.org/wiki/Soccer_mom

CPSIA information can be obtained
at www.ICGtesting.com
Printed in the USA
FSOW04n0131140917
38483FS